THE POTTER'S HOUSE

THE POTTER'S HOUSE

REV. WALLACE H. HEFLIN

Destiny Image Publishers
P.O. Box 351
Shippensburg, PA 17257

**"Speaking to the Purposes of God
for this Generation"**

ISBN 0-914903-91-8

For Worldwide Distribution
Printed in the U.S.A.

Special Thanks to Mrs. Melda Marvel for her hard work in preparing this manuscript and to Dorothy Erdman for typing.

*T*he word which came to Jeremiah from the Lord, saying, Arise, and go down to the potter's house, and there I will cause thee to hear My words.

*T*hen I went down to the potter's house, and, behold, he wrought a work on the wheels.

*A*nd the vessel that he made of clay was marred in the hand of the potter: so he made it again another vessel, as seemed good to the potter to make it.

*T*hen the Word of the Lord came to me, saying,

O House of Israel, cannot I do with you as this potter? saith the Lord. Behold, as the clay is in the potter's hand, so are ye in Mine hand, O house of Israel.

*A*t what instant I shall speak concerning a nation, and concerning a kingdom, to pluck up, and to pull down, and to destroy it;

*I*f that nation, against whom I have pronounced, turn from their evil, I will repent of the evil that I thought to do unto them.

And at what instant I shall speak concerning a nation, and concerning a kingdom, to build and to plant it;

If it do evil in My sight, that it obey not My voice, then I will repent of the good, wherewith I said I would benefit them.

Now therefore go to, speak to the men of Judah, and to the inhabitants of Jerusalem, saying, Thus saith the Lord; Behold, I frame evil against you, and devise a device against you: return ye now every one from his evil way, and make your ways and your doings good.

(Jeremiah 18:1-11)

Contents

Introduction

In Kota, India, in 1970 I had the privilege of visiting a potter's house. It made a great impact on my life. As I watched the potter at work and listened to him describe the process through which the clay is taken, from the difficult job of digging it out to applying the finishing touches, I could see the hand of God at work.

As I read God's Word describing Jeremiah's visit to the potter's house, I realized the many things we still need to learn. God is the Master Potter. He desires to make something beautiful of each of us. But, a long process—involving acquiring the clay, cleansing it, preparing it, separating it, forming it, perfecting it, firing it and beautifying it—is necessary to bring forth the final product that only He can visualize.

Sometimes we feel that nothing is happening in our spiritual lives. We wonder why we are not experiencing the same things as others. But, we may be in different stages of the Master's work. Each process is different and yet necessary to the final beauty of the vessel He wants to create. I want you to be able to say, "God is working on me. He has me on the wheel. He is changing me."

The cry of my heart through the years has been to be the vessel that God could use. I believe you feel the same way. We just need to identify what God is doing in us and then cooperate with Him to make the process less painful and more productive. The final verses of the text show us that God can change a nation in an *"instant."* If He can change a whole nation in an instant, don't you think He can change you? I know He can. Let's take a trip together—to *The Potter's House.*

Chapter One

God Speaks

There I will cause thee to hear My words.
(Jeremiah 18:2)

God sent Jeremiah to the potter's house so that He could speak to Him further. God wanted to teach Jeremiah about the process of forming vessels so that he could take the message to the people of Judah. God hasn't changed. Thank God, He's still speaking to men and women today. And, thank God, there are still those who can hear His voice. Many cannot because they are not listening, but God hasn't stopped speaking. He is ready to speak to every one of us. God will speak to you while you are cooking dinner, while you are mending a fence, while you are doing your homework or while you are driving down the road.

He is speaking in dreams and visions. He is speaking through His Word. He is speaking through tongues and interpretation and other gifts of the Spirit. But, more and more He is speaking through His prophets. The ministry of prophets is not over. It is just beginning. And you cannot be a prophet until you first let God work in you and until you can hear His voice.

"My sheep hear my voice," Jesus said (John 10:27). We need to hear from God and be guided by His voice. We jump into things and then expect the Lord to bail us out when we get in trouble. If we were hearing His voice more, He wouldn't have to bail us out so much.

The world doesn't need just another prophet, another preacher. The world needs to hear "thus saith the Lord." They won't always like what they hear. Jeremiah was thrown into prison when he delivered his message. The king preferred the message of the false prophets to the truth of God. But, Jeremiah didn't compromise. When the king sent servants to the dungeon to ask Jeremiah one day, "Is there any message from God?" Jeremiah answered back, "Yes, the same message I already gave you" (See Jeremiah 21). God doesn't change His mind.

It costs something to be a prophet. It costs something to be a man or woman of God. It costs something to stand for righteousness and purity and holiness. It costs something to walk this old-fashioned way. It costs something to stand for right and against wrong. If you are willing to pay that price, God is ready to speak to you and call you up higher.

First, God told Jeremiah to *"arise."* You will never have the full revelation of what God has for you until you arise from the position you are in. You are not going to receive any greater revelation than you have already until you come up higher—"arise."

We don't understand sometimes why others hear from God and get such great revelations. It is because they have moved forward in God. When God has given us all He can in one level of anointing, we must move on into a new depth in Him. He hasn't run out of revelation. But, we must be enlarged to receive more.

"Is this scriptural?" someone may ask.

Jesus hand-picked, called and anointed His disciples. They went out to work for Him. They preached, healed the sick, cast out demons, and prepared the way for His entrance into all the villages. Yet in John 16:12 and 13, He said to them, *"I have yet many things to say unto you, but ye cannot bear them now. Howbeit when He, the Spirit of Truth is come, He will guide you into all truth...."*

There are many different levels of revelation. God speaks to us according to the depth we have reached in Him. When Jesus said to those who were following Him, *"...Except ye eat the flesh of the Son of Man, and drink His blood, ye have no life in you"* (John 6:53), they answered, *"...This is an hard saying; who can hear it"* (Verse 60)? The Scripture records, *"From that time many of His disciples went back, and walked no more with Him"* (Verse 66). Those disciples could not receive the greater revelation Jesus was trying to give them because of the level of their spiritual commitment.

The writer of Hebrews stated, *"...When for the time ye ought to be teachers, ye have need that one teach you again which be the first principles of the oracles of God; and are become such as have need of milk, and not of strong meat"* (Hebrews 5:12).

"Arise," he was telling them, "come up higher. Come into a new level. You've been in that present level long enough." It's time to move on, grow up in God. When we take a new step in God, He gives us greater truths, deeper revelations, and we are enlarged. But, it can only happen in your life if you arise and move forward.

The closer we get to Heaven, the more God is revealing to us about Heaven. We know more about Heaven now than was known two or three hundred years ago, not because He wasn't revealing His secrets in those days. He was, but only in measure. We see *"through a glass, darkly"* (I Corinthians 13:12), but the closer we get to home, the clearer the vision becomes.

A bridegroom who plans to take his bride to another place will, as the time grows near, begin to tell her more and more about her new home. If he plans to move to North Carolina, for example, he begins to tell her about hush puppies, barbecue, corn bread and grits. A man who will soon return to Virginia with his bride begins to tell her about country fried chicken and Virginia ham.

The Heavenly Bridegroom is revealing to His Bride mysteries that have been hidden in ages past. The scales are being removed from our eyes so that we might see the greater things that God is anxiously waiting to show us. These are the greatest days ever for the revelation of God, but there must be an enlargement in us so that we can contain the revelations He wants to give. Paul told the Corinthians, *"But God hath revealed them unto us by his Spirit"* (I Corinthians 2:10). RISE UP!

Some folks might say, "I'm just a homebody. I don't like to go anywhere." Get ready to travel.

Amen! Get ready. God has another home waiting for us. We're on a journey. We are pilgrims and strangers here. We won't be staying here very long. Don't get too comfortable.

The children of Israel could have stayed in Egypt. Egypt was all they knew. It was home for them. But, they were told to be ready when the trumpet sounded. The custom was to blow two blasts with a ram's horn, called a shofar. The first blast was a signal to take down the goat skin tent, pack up the utensils and make all the necessary preparations for travel. The second shofar sounded marching orders.

We are sounding the first trumpet announcing that we must get ready to move. We are going home. When the last trumpet sounds, there will be no time to get ready. We will depart in an instant—if we are ready. Make up your mind to go. Arise!

Half the joy of going somewhere is the journey itself. Some folks say, "Pray for me that I might endure." I am not just enduring. I am enjoying the journey. True, there are some mountains to climb and some valleys to cross, but I'm enjoying it all. I enjoy crossing the mountains just as much as I do the level places. Mountains are beautiful. I want you to enjoy the journey. No one is forcing me to make this journey. I am not "peculiar" just because my church has legislated it that way. I am in this way because I want to be in this way. I am shouting the victory and enjoying the ride—all the way home. Arise and go!

God told Joshua to arise and cross the Jordan River. He could have stayed on the other side. It was more familiar to him. But, he never would have possessed what was his. God told him, *"Go over this Jordan"* (Joshua 1:2).

If we keep our spiritual ears open, the Holy Ghost will speak to us in many ways throughout the day and even when we are sleeping. David received counsel of the Lord *"...in the night seasons"* (Psalms 16:7). As we are obedient to the voice of God and go forth, the Holy Ghost takes us by the hand and leads us through the paths that bring us into different levels in God.

A small Christian radio station here beside the camp broadcasts twenty-four hours a day. If I am not tuned into their frequency, however, I can't hear them—even though they are broadcasting. God can speak to you wherever you are. Just begin to recognize the ways that He speaks. Get tuned into His frequency.

God took the prophet Ezekiel by the hand and led him out into the waters. He got up to his ankles, then to his knees and then to his loins. God wasn't measuring the waters. He knew how deep they were. He was measuring the prophet. The Spirit of God is taking us by the hand and leading us out into deeper waters. He loves to get us out so deep that we can't touch bottom. He wants us to depend on Him. But, He never leaves us alone in that deep water. He has promised, *"I will never leave thee, nor forsake thee"* (Hebrews 13:5). He will be there.

It all begins when we arise and go. Many want to arise, but never go anywhere. It's time to go. It really doesn't matter where God sends us. He has promised to be with us and that wherever we put the soles of our feet we may possess the land. He has anointed our feet, and wherever we go we can claim the land we tread on for Him. How can you tread on lands for God if you don't first arise and go?

Jeremiah could have questioned God, "What can You tell me at the potter's house that You can't tell me here at home?" My visit to the potter's house was an exciting experience for me. We buy our cookware and tableware at department stores. We have Revereware with copper clad bottoms, waterless and greaseless cookware by West Bend Aluminum, Wearever and Club Aluminum and so many other good brands. I had never seen a potter at work. But, a visit to the potter's house was nothing exciting for Jeremiah. No doubt he had been to the potter's house many times and was familiar with what was done there. Every village had a potter. Those people obtained their household vessels at the potter's house. A visit to the potter's house was nothing new to him.

But, Jeremiah didn't argue with God or question His judgment. He had learned, as we all should, that God has a purpose in everything that He says and does. When He says, "Go," we need to start moving. And when He says, "Stay," we should not step foot outside the door. If we can learn the secret of divine direction just by letting God speak to us, we will be so much better off. Jeremiah arose and went to the potter's house.

What did God want to show Jeremiah at the potter's house? He wanted Jeremiah to see how the potter was working with the clay, so he could understand the way He was working with the House of Israel. In the same way that a potter works with the clay, so Jesus, the Master Potter, is working with each of us every day. The more pliable we are in His hands the more quickly and easily He can make of us a vessel of honor for His glory. He puts us through all the same processes that the clay passes through.

The House of God is, in many ways, the potter's house. When we go to church, we're going to the potter's house to let the Master Potter form something new of us. Many churches do not encourage or permit the molding and fashioning of the Lord. No pressure is ever applied to the clay. We are made to feel "comfortable," nothing more. But, God doesn't want us to go in the door and come back out unchanged. He wants to change us into His likeness and His image. Without change there can be no growth in God. Anything that isn't growing and changing is probably already dead. God wants to see His people grow. Not a single day should pass without some type of spiritual change in our lives.

Preaching about the potter's house one night in Australia, I began by saying, "I want to take you folks down to the potter's house so that the Lord can speak to you."

After the service a man came to me and said, "We attend a different church. We weren't planning to come here tonight. About five o'clock God told us to come. When you said that you were going to speak about the potter's house, I knew that God was going to do something for my family. You see, our name is Potter. That's my wife over there and she isn't saved. She needs to get saved and filled with the Holy Ghost."

We went over to Mrs. Potter and laid hands on her, and she got saved and filled with the Holy Ghost. When the Potter children saw what was happening to their mother, they began to weep. They were filled with the Holy Ghost as well. God also filled a teenaged girl whom they had brought with them.

Brother Potter had, until then, held an important position in the agricultural sector in Australia, but a few months later he and his family accompanied another minister to the mission fields of South Africa. The Potter house was changed in the Potter's House.

We should be living so that God can speak to us just as specifically wherever we are—although we know He does special things *"where two or three are gathered"* (Matthew 18:20). If we listen we will realize that the Lord is speaking to us as He did to Jeremiah, *"Arise, and go down to the potter's house, and there I will cause thee to hear My words."*

Chapter Two

The Digging

He brought me up also out of an horrible pit, out of the miry clay, and set my feet upon a rock, and established my goings. (Psalms 40:2)

The potter knows his clay. He knows what he can make if he has the right materials. He goes to great lengths to acquire the clay before he can ever think of forming a vessel. I saw the place where the potter found the best clay. It was the back-waters of a river. The tides came in, bringing with them much debris. Then, as the water receded a deposit of debris—which eventually became very deep—was left on top of the clay. The potter had to free the clay from this prison. With great effort he dug away the trash to discover the hidden treasure beneath.

That clay didn't look very valuable to me. It didn't look worth the effort necessary to get it out. I might have said, "It's useless, worthless." Maybe someone has said that about you. But, the Potter doesn't see you as you are, but as what you can become with His help.

Clay doesn't seem to be very cooperative with the potter either. The best clay produces a natural suction that resists every effort to pry it loose. It resists being separated from the rest of the clay. Our God patiently digs us out of the miry clay and establishes our feet upon the Rock. Isaiah said, *"Hearken to me, ye that follow after righteousness, ye that seek the Lord: look unto the rock whence ye are hewn, and to the hole of the pit whence ye are digged"* (Isaiah 51:1).

God blesses us so much that sometimes we forget where we came from and the things we used to do. When we see someone else doing those things, we're not as sympathetic toward them as we should be. We must remember the pit we came from.

Just as there is a suction to the miry clay, the devil has his hand on sinners and tries to hold them fast and not let them go. Drunkards who are on the verge of salvation sometimes go on the worst drunk just before they yield themselves to Christ. The enemy doesn't want to let them go. It is easier for teenagers (who have been in sin just a short time) to be delivered than it is for those who have been in sin for thirty-five or forty years. These people are bound with many chords. Just a gentle prayer will not bring their deliverance. We need to fast and pray for them. As we do, one by one those bondages are broken, and a great release comes from the pit.

One sister in North Carolina prayed for twelve years for her husband to get saved. She began to wonder if God would ever save him, but she continued to pray. One day as her husband came in the door from work, he said, "I want to get saved."

"What did you say?" she asked.

"I said I want to get saved," he repeated. "If you don't help me I'm going to call Brother Heflin and make him come down here and help me." He got saved, and she felt like she was saved all over again.

Never give up on sinners. Hold firm for them until the victory comes. It will come. I ran from God for twenty-nine years. My mother fasted one hundred and eight and a half days and my father fasted one hundred and ten days, drinking only a little liquid, and prayed for me day and night. One by one those chains that were wrapped around me were broken, and I was brought out of that horrible pit into which I had fallen. It was after ninety days of his fast that I got saved. He was determined not to put another morsel of solid food in his mouth until I was free. That was a big order for his stubborn and rebellious son, but he was determined that I would not go to hell. The Word says, *"The effectual fervent prayer of a righteous man availeth much"* (James 5:16).

My father himself was saved through the same kind of determined and persistent prayer. Mother fell in love with him before she ever knew him and before he ever got saved. Some members of the church had asked that his name be put on the prayer list. He was a sinner. He needed God. As Mother prayed for him every day, she began to sense the greatness of what God wanted to do through Wallace Heflin. And she prayed until he got saved and became a preacher of righteousness.

We Christians have the only Savior who goes out searching for the lost. That was His reason for coming into the world. *"For the Son of Man is come to seek and to save that which was lost"* (Luke 19:10). In the false religions and false cults, it is the lost who must search after the religion. Hindu worshipers in India take pilgrimages of more than a thousand miles in search of the blessings of their gods. They neglect business and family to search for the truth. An annual pilgrimage is made to a Lake formed by the Pushka River. They believe that bathing only once in that holy river washes away all their sins. Thousands of them travel, carrying a few possessions and meager food supplies on their heads. As I watched them immerse themselves in the water, I could sense their expectancy. As they departed, however, another spirit was detected. Expectancy had given place to disappointment.

Thank God that our Savior is the Good Shepherd who doesn't rest when most of the sheep are safe. He goes out into the night in search of the lost one. Our Lord is digging for treasure hidden by rubbish. He doesn't find it sitting in church. He finds it out there covered with the dregs of society. No matter how deep sinners are mired, He sees their potential and has a plan and purpose for each of them. He will go to whatever depths are necessary to bring up the clay.

If God has gone to such lengths to find and dig us out, He must know something we don't know. He sees a value we haven't been able to see. He has a vision we have not yet glimpsed. He sees us, not as we are, but as we can become. Because only He has that vision, only He can form us into that perfected vessel. We are still nothing without Him. With His help we become something beautiful. But, the process is just beginning.

Chapter Three

The Washing

Unto Him that loved us, and washed us from our sins in His own blood. (Revelation 1:5)

After the potter has dug the clay from the river and transported it to his house, he begins the lengthy washing process necessary to remove all the debris from it. It will be rinsed many times before he is satisfied that all the pollution brought in by the tides is gone, and the clay is pure. The world has left a deposit on our souls and something has to happen to remove it. This is not something that you can do for yourself, but God has made provision for our cleansing. The angel Gabriel said to Joseph, *"...Thou shalt call His name Jesus: for He shall save His people from their sins" (Matthew 1:21).* That was His purpose in coming. He is in the saving business.

Everyone must go through this same cleansing process. Even if you have been considered a kind, sweet and tender person, you need the same cleansing as the person who has plunged to the depths of sin. We are all sinners in God's sight.

My mother was saved when she was just a young girl and never knew what it was to be in the world. Once she was in Colonial Beach with my father conducting a revival. Colonial Beach was known as "Little Reno." Buildings on the Virginia side projected out into the waters of Maryland because Maryland had open drinking and gambling, while Virginia did not. She decided that she wanted to see how "the other half" lived. After service was over one evening, she walked up a ramp, with my father and sister, into one of those buildings. She saw the smoke-filled rooms with the one-armed bandits along one wall. She saw the drinking, the dancing and everything else that was going on there. Because she had lived such a sheltered life, she couldn't believe what she was seeing. Although she had never been contaminated by "the world of sin," she had been a sinner and, as a child, recognized her need of Jesus as Savior. We all need to do it.

Thank God for the shed blood of Jesus. *"...Without* [the] *shedding of blood* [there] *is no remission"* (Hebrews 9:22). He came to save us "from" our sins. He washes our souls in His blood, and its cleansing and purifying power removes all the stains of sin.

There is a concerted effort in some Christian circles to avoid any mention of the blood. Teaching of the blood is thought to promote a "slaughter-house religion." "It is unnecessary," they say. Some versions of the Bible have removed references to the blood, and songs about the blood have been removed from many modern song books. It is because leaders no longer believe in the efficacy of the blood of the crucified Christ and its power to redeem sinners. They, like Cain, are offering to God a bloodless sacrifice.

But, we still sing those old songs:

Would you be free from your burden of sin?
There's power in the blood,
power in the blood.
Would you o'er evil a victory win?
There's wonderful power in the blood.

Chorus
There is power, power,
wonder-working power
In the blood of the Lamb.

There is power, power,
wonder-working power
In the precious blood of the Lamb.

There is a fountain filled with blood
Drawn from Emmanuel's veins
And sinners plunged beneath that blood
Lose all their guilty stains

Have you been to Jesus for the cleansing power?
Are you washed in the blood of the Lamb?
There's a fountain flowing for the soul unclean.
Oh, be washed in the blood of the Lamb.

Chorus
Are you washed in the blood,
In the soul-cleansing blood of the Lamb?
Are your garments spotless?
Are they white as snow?
Are you washed in the blood of the Lamb?

What can wash away my sins?
Nothing but the blood of Jesus.
What can make me whole again?
Nothing but the blood of Jesus.

Chorus
Oh, precious is the flow

that makes me white as snow.
No other fount I know.
Nothing but the blood of Jesus.

Just as I am without one plea,
But that Thy blood was shed for me.
And that Thou bidst me come to Thee.
Oh, Lamb of God, I come.

I always loved to hear someone sing that song that says, *"Each drop of blood bought me a million years."* Don't ever be ashamed of the precious blood that redeemed us.

We agree that we don't need the bulls, or heifers, or turtle doves. Animal sacrifice cannot take away the sins of the human race. But, the precious blood of the only begotten Son of the Father has never lost its power. He was willing to leave the ivory places of glory that our souls might be delivered from the bondages of sin and that we might be like Him.

Many churches refuse to contend for old-fashioned salvation for their new converts. Because they are anxious to count the numbers, time is not given for the blood to do its work. Often a sinner's prayer is repeated, and the people go out the door to light up a cigarette and go on living the way they've always lived. The blood of Jesus has no chance to do its office work.

Another sad practice among some believers is casting demons out of each other. A demon has no right to dwell in a blood-washed believer. What they're trying to cast out are the works of the flesh. That should have been taken care of when the person got saved, and it would have been done if they had allowed the cleansing of the Lord to take place in their lives. These teachings tend to make the experience God has given us of no effect. We must contend for the washing of the blood of Jesus. Peter called it, *"the precious blood of Christ"* (I Peter 1:19).

Everything we get from God is a direct result of His shedding *"the precious blood."* We're not only saved by His blood, we are also healed by His blood, and we are sanctified by His blood. He was beaten with many stripes and wounded in many parts of His body. Blood flowed from those wounds so that you and I might have life and have it more abundantly. The Master Potter washes our souls with that blood, and the miracle of cleansing takes place.

This washing in the blood will even make a drunkard sober. A man came into one of my services reeking so strongly of alcohol that everyone turned to see who had come in the door. He had to get drunk to get up his nerve to go to church. As the service progressed, God drew him and he went forward to be prayed for. We laid hands on him and the Spirit of God began to wash him from the crown of his head to the soles of his feet. He stood there weeping his way to Jesus. Then, suddenly I realized I could no longer smell the alcohol, even when he blew his breath directly in my face.

As God said, *"...Old things are passed away; behold, all things are become new"* (II Corinthians 5:17). Jesus had washed him and cleaned him up. When he went home even his old dog was aware that something had happened to him that day. Never be ashamed of the fact that we believe in the redeeming power of *"the precious blood"* of Jesus.

My Mother has always believed that none of the blood was lost, that angels were present to catch it as it came from the hands, the feet, the side and the brow of our Lord. I felt she was right. On a visit to Lisbon, Portugal, we were touring one of the famous museums. As we moved from one room to another, viewing the beautiful works of art, a large and ancient oil painting of the crucifixion caught my attention. It extended from the ceiling to the floor and was dated 1535. The artist who painted it had received a revelation from God. Under each hand he had painted an angel catching the blood of

Jesus. Another angel was catching the blood from His side, and still another was catching the blood from His feet.

On the resurrection morning, Mary, seeing Jesus alive, wanted to touch Him, but He said, *"Touch me not; for I am not yet ascended to My Father: but go to My brethren, and say unto them, I ascend unto My Father, and your Father; and to My God, and your God"* (John 20:17). He then ascended into heaven and took the blood, His own *"precious blood,"* and personally delivered it to the Tabernacle of Heaven. Now, when the Father looks down upon us, He no longer sees us in our unrighteousness. He Looks through the veil of the blood of His Son and sees us—on the other side of that blood—pure and holy, redeemed through that great sacrifice. How wonderful the experience! And how blessed we are that Jesus loved us enough to be willing to give Himself for our redemption. Thank you Master Potter.

Paul experienced a total transformation. The things he had loved he now hated. His entire life was turned upside down. The message he had hated he now risked his life to preach. His was a total transformation. We can resist the cleansing of the Lord and hold on to things of the flesh. But if we do, we will be the loser.

The day I got saved I stayed on my knees weeping for more than an hour. I was so sorry for my sins. I saw my nothingness and His righteousness. Deliverance came as His blood was applied to my heart. When I got up from there, I wanted to live a life committed to God. When we serve the devil, we do everything he wants us to. Why not feel the same way about Jesus? Let Him have all; give Him your heart, your soul and your energies. Give the Master Potter a chance to work and prove what He can make of your life.

This still works. You don't have to keep sucking cigarettes, and drinking whiskey, doing drugs, chasing women and all the other things you used to do. When Jesus comes in, those desires go out. You are delivered by the power of Almighty God.

Just before I got saved I was buying four packs of cigarettes a day. I smoked three of them and kept the fourth one to be sure I didn't run out in the middle of the night. Yes, I had become concerned about my health, and like so many, I was trying to cut back. So, I was smoking cigars and a pipe. But, from the moment that Jesus came into my life, I've never desired another cigarette, another cigar, or another pipe. Jesus lives in me, and He doesn't smoke.

I have heard some professing Christians trying to explain away their bad habits by saying, "I haven't gotten sanctified yet." I am wondering if they even got saved. If Jesus is living in us, we should be taking on His nature. Can you imagine

Him doing some of the things professing Christians are doing?

Across our country many preachers are now having wine with their meals and are justifying it by saying, "It's all right because Jesus turned the water into wine." The Apostle Paul said, *"For if I build again the things which I destroyed, I make myself a transgressor"* (Galatians 2:18). When you return to sin, you become a sinner all over again. That means you need to go back to that fountain that Zechariah saw opened *"to the house of David...for sin and for uncleanness"* (Zechariah 13:1). Allow the Master Potter to wash you and cleanse you afresh and to make of you the vessel that God would have you to be.

During the "Jesus Movement" of the sixties, Ruth and I were in California and witnessed a large gathering of young people drawn to that movement. We saw many of them on the streets of Los Angeles "witnessing." Many were barefooted, the women wearing tank tops, the long-haired men wearing the typical bands around their heads. Many of them were smoking openly. They spent seven and eight hours every day out there "representing God." Ruth sat there that afternoon and wept. All she could say was, "Jesus, You deserve better. Jesus, You deserve better than this to represent You. Jesus, You deserve better than this to represent You."

What was happening? Those young people had been doing the drug scene. They were promoting free love. You name it and they were doing it. But, they were also genuinely looking for an answer, and Jesus was that answer. The church people that got involved in winning them, however, were so anxious to get numbers that they did not raise any standard and say, "This is what God requires. If you want what I have, this is the price you must pay." They let them go on living their ungodly lifestyle.

I personally believe those young people would have paid the price. They would have stayed under the fountain of the blood until a cleansing and purification had taken place—if they had known there was more. They were zealous. While most preachers were afraid to preach the second coming of the Lord, news magazines were carrying pictures and accounts of those young people with placards raised high declaring, *"Jesus is coming soon."*

In the end, the "Jesus People" did not have what was necessary to remain faithful when the storms of persecution began to blow. It wasn't long before that great movement began to dissipate. Why? Because no one had the courage to say to them, "You must stay in God's presence long enough for the washing and the purifying of the Holy Ghost to take place in your soul."

Even many Pentecostal churches no longer allow the washing of the Word to take its course. As a result, they are not seeing what God's Spirit and power can produce with miry clay.

We must do something about the many people who go to church and invite Jesus into their hearts, then go back and live the same life they were living before. They sit in churches in that condition and wonder why God isn't using them. I don't think they are entirely to blame. We are responsible to see that they allow the blood to do its cleansing work. The washing begins the purifying work of sanctification and holiness.

God doesn't take everything away from us, as some believe. He cleanses what we have and redirects it for His glory. Peter was just as impetuous for the Lord as he had been in his former life. If you are energized for the devil, you can be a dynamo for God.

The moment Jesus comes in and saves us there is a definite work of sanctification that takes place. The old desires, the cravings and longings go. However, that isn't the end of His working us over. He will also do a progressive work in our lives, if we let Him. If God had required of me the day I got saved what He requires of me now, I couldn't have made it. I have grown in grace. It is a daily process. Paul said, *"I die daily"* (I Corinthians 15:31). We *"grow in grace, and in the knowledge of our Lord and Saviour Jesus Christ"* (II Peter 3:18), preparing ourselves for the things that we will face.

Sanctification is such an important work. Not only does the blood sanctify, the Father sanctifies; the Son sanctifies; the Holy Ghost sanctifies; and the Word sanctifies. Nothing is left to chance. No area is left untouched. No weapon or tool is left unused in the effort to make His people into treasured vessels.

Great quantities of water are used by the potter to keep his clay clean. It will be washed and washed again. Debris prevents the potter from forming a vessel. It must go. Let Him wash you well.

Often we act as though the washing, the cleansing, is the last step. That is just the beginning. Yet, some churches preach nothing else. If you attend their services, you get fifty-seven varieties of salvation served, but nothing else. This is just one step toward maturity. Salvation is just a key that unlocks the treasures of God. This is only an open door. Now, we must enter. This is only the beginning of what God has in store for us. There is certainly nothing wrong with preaching salvation; but there is so much more that needs to be preached.

Many people want to stop with the washing because nothing much is expected of them. They have fewer problems, fewer challenges. Many people have never ever been persecuted; and they like it that way. Many have never borne a burden; and they like it that way.

Just because you are washed does not make you a useful vessel. Don't be satisfied just to be clean. God wants to form you and perfect you and use you.

Chapter Four

The Drying

*Because the creature itself also shall be
delivered from the bondage of corruption into
the glorious liberty of the children of God.*
(Romans 8:21)

After we are cleansed, there is a period in which
the Lord leaves us for a time to dry out. We simply
bask in the sun—as it were—enjoying "the glorious
liberty." It is a wonderful period, and we hate for
it to end. Salvation is wonderful! Everything is
new and right with the world! We love everybody!
If we don't move beyond this stage, however,
we will never be the majestic vessels the Lord

envisions. Get ready, problems are coming, and they are coming for our benefit.

We often leave new converts in this stage. We are so happy they have been cleansed that we forget they are not mature yet. They are not strong yet. They are not formed yet. They are not useful vessels yet. Clay that is washed is just wet clay. If something is not done with that clay, what good does it serve? The process is only beginning.

They may be forty-five years old, but they are babes. They are in a very vulnerable stage. We cannot leave them to fend for themselves. If an infant is abandoned at birth, it will die within a very short period. The spiritual life isn't any different. Spiritual infants have been born again, but they need constant care. And not much can be expected of them. They eat, they sleep, they love to cuddle in mother's arms. They need time to mature. And we must nurture them. They have all the attributes of a complete individual. But, much of it is promise, not reality.

New believers testify with fire. They have great joy, great love etc. But they have a lot of sorting out to do. They don't know much yet, and are very limited in what they can actually do. God has ordained us to go forth and *"bring forth fruit"* and that our *"fruit should remain"* (John 15:16). We have a responsibility to see that the fruit is not lost.

God does not dig us from the miry clay and wash us just so we can be saved and on our way to heaven. He saves us that we might be of service. He has only our hands and our feet and our mouths to be extensions of Himself and do the work that He started when He was here. All the steps He puts us through are for the purpose of preparing us to be greater servants in His kingdom. Some of the steps are painful, but necessary. The Potter knows best.

As Christians, we are never really satisfied unless we are giving ourselves to God in service. Clay which has not become a useful vessel is just clay. People who have the most emotional problems are those who shut themselves in and never give of themselves. When we are giving of ourselves to others, we see that many people have greater problems than we do. The whole process that the potter goes through is not a punishment to the clay. His desire is for the clay to fulfill its potential.

Many of us are satisfied to stay in the drying out stage. When things start to go wrong, we are almost convinced that we have lost something, that we have backslidden. We are not anxious to submit ourselves to the mixing, the molding, the firing, the adorning etc. But God is anxious to get on with the making of the vessel. He will begin just as soon as the clay can stand it. Everything He is about to do is for the good of the clay. One of the most difficult steps on the road to perfection is about to begin—the beating.

Chapter Five

The Beating

For our light affliction, which is but for a moment, worketh for us a far more exceeding and eternal weight of glory.

(II Corinthians 4:17)

When the clay is completely dry, the potter places it on a table and, using a long flat stick, begins to beat it. With such care he dug it out. With such care he cleansed it. Now he beats it mercilessly. But, he is not doing that just for fun. He is doing it to get out all the lumps. He cannot mold clay filled with lumps. A brick mason cannot work with lumpy mortar. It throws his work off and wastes much of his valuable time. None of us like lumps. Who likes to eat lumpy mashed potatoes? Who likes to sleep in a bed with lumps in it? God has to get the lumps out of you to make you into something pleasant.

The other reason the potter beats the clay is that certain impurities are hidden deep within and only become apparent or come to the surface in the beating process. As he beats the dried clay, he finds these impurities—small pebbles, sticks, and trash. As he encounters them, He carefully lifts them out and throws them aside, then continues his beating. And this is no short process.

If the potter is unconcerned about the quality of the vessels he will produce, he may shorten this step. If, however, he is commissioned to produce the most exquisite pots available, the beating process takes much longer. Nothing must hinder the perfection of the vessel.

That drying out period seems wonderful. Everything seems to be going our way. We have the world on a string. House payments and car payments come in days ahead of time. We wish we had known all along how great salvation was. When the drying out period has ended, however, the fun begins. The enemy comes along with his trials and tribulations. The beating begins.

Just because you got saved doesn't mean you are perfect. Most of us have a long way to go. There is much in us that is not pleasing to the Potter. When Jesus said, *"Be ye therefore perfect, even as your Father which is in heaven is perfect"* (Matthew 5:48), He was setting a goal for us, an ideal. It may take us a long time to fully attain that goal.

Yes! The Word tells us, *"Therefore leaving the principles of the doctrine of Christ, let us go on unto perfection; not laying again the foundation of repentance from dead works, and of faith toward God, of the doctrine of baptisms, and of laying on of hands, and of resurrection of the dead, and of eternal judgment. And this will we do, if God permit"* (Hebrews 6:1-3). There is nothing wrong with these foundational truths; but, we need to go on to other things. You don't do that in a day. It takes time. It is part of the process.

The Lord is there to say, "I don't want you to do **that** anymore. I don't want you to wear **that** anymore. I don't want you to say **that** anymore. I want you to start doing **this**," etc. Oh, does it hurt to see the lumps we have. Is it easier to be less perfect? Probably. But if you choose to remain imperfect, you will never be the vessel God wants. You will tie the hands of God, so that He cannot use you as He intended. If the Lord works on you, it means that He loves you. Does the Word not say, *"For whom the Lord loveth He chasteneth, and scourgeth every son whom He receiveth"*

(Hebrews 12:6)? Don't resist His work. Thank Him for it.

The Master Potter is not satisfied simply to get out the lumps. He beats the clay until it becomes a fine powder, the finer the better. And the finer the powder becomes the more easily impurities are detected and removed. Isn't this just the way the Master Potter works with us?

The beatings we undergo don't seem pleasant to us at the time, but they do refine us and make us fit for forming into a vessel of honor. None of us like to be beaten; but the longer we resist the longer it takes to become material He can use. The quicker we respond to the beating the less beating it takes to prepare us. How long do I have to be beaten? As long as lumps remain.

We always think it's the devil who's beating us. Sometimes it is—but only with the Lord's permission. He cannot touch us unless God foresees that what he is doing will work something good in us. The potter may occasionally permit someone else to beat the clay. He oversees the work, however, and is always sure that it is being done correctly. Your family may be beating you. Your spouse may be beating you. But, God is permitting that. He is perfecting His Bride. When He finds in us those little pebbles and those lumps, He must remove them so that we can be perfected. He keeps working on us until the hardness of our spirit is removed.

Even preachers are guilty of having a hard spirit. Some evangelists have such a hardness in their spirit that people cannot receive from them. The compassion of Christ isn't there. They want to minister to people quickly so they can go home. When we are moved with compassion and a person stands before us for prayer, often they are healed before we ever touch them. God anoints a soft spirit. When there is hardness in the spirit of the minister, the person being ministered to can sense it. They know that you don't really care about them, that you want to hurry and get rid of them so you can pray for someone else.

Sometimes, even when great miracles are happening in a service, we get tired and begin to rush things, and the needs of the people are not met. We can't rush God. We have to wait upon Him, and let the anointing flow. When we do, the needs are met and those same people are not back in the line the next service.

Many people who want to serve the Lord cannot because they have such a hard spirit. He wants us to be more like Him. He brings pressure to bear on us and sends, and permits the devil to send, trials our way to bring us into a spiritual tenderness. Some of us don't want others to know there is a tender side of us. But why not? Christ was tender and compassionate. The writer of Hebrews declares, *"For we have not an high priest which cannot be touched with the feeling of our infirmities; but was in all points tempted like as we are, yet without sin"* (Hebrews 4:15). If His compassion is to flow through us, our spirit must change. We must be able to feel the needs of others and the responsibility to meet that need.

Some ministers who once had a powerful anointing seem to have become ineffective in meeting the needs of the people. They arrive at a service just in time to minister and leave as soon as they have finished. Others, after they have become successful, turn to answering services and unlisted telephone numbers so that no one can reach them. They thus make themselves inaccessible to the very people who need their ministry. One good friend, a well-known national evangelist, is wonderful in this regard. It never matters to him how many hours he has been praying for people or how tired he is, he always greets those who approach him as though they were long lost relatives.

Never get so busy and pressured that you allow yourself to become untouchable. Don't give way to that hardness of spirit. If you do, it will hinder the compassion of Christ from flowing out of you to meet the needs of God's people. Paul said, *"...I keep under my body, and bring it into subjection: lest that by any means, when I have preached to others, I myself should be a castaway"* (I Corinthians 9:27). He didn't mean he was in danger of losing his salvation. He meant that God wouldn't use him anymore.

We must always remember that wherever we go we represent the Lord. We are a vessel that contains His anointing, and we are not our own. Therefore, we must let Him continue His work in us until He is satisfied that we are the vessel on which He can put His stamp of approval.

My Mother has often said, "Son, you have to win them to yourself before you can win them to Christ." It is true. I must be like Him.

This process is so much easier if we volunteer ourselves to be worked over. The Word says, *"And whosoever shall fall on this stone shall be broken: but on whomsoever it shall fall, it will grind him to powder"* (Matthew 21:44). The quicker we become submissive and let Him break our head-strong will the sooner His desires will come forth. He is more anxious than we are to stop the beatings and get on with the process. He knows what He can make of us. But, He cannot stop until we have the required softness.

Chapter Six

The Sifting

I will sift the house of Israel among all nations, like as corn is sifted in a sieve.... (Amos 9:9)

Simon, Simon, behold, Satan hath desired to have you, that he may sift you as wheat: (Luke 22:31)

When the clay was pulverized sufficiently, the potter began to sift it through a very fine screen. Some elements, though quite small, would not pass through the screen. If they were impurities, the potter cast them aside. If, however, they were simply lumps that had not yet been worked out, they were placed back on the table for more beating. Why didn't he just throw them away? He knew their value. This clay was purchased with a great price. It was valuable. It was not to be tossed aside lightly. Every opportunity must be given to the clay to produce. He beat it some more.

We often think we have been beaten and worked over until there could not possibly be more lumps left in us. But, when the sifting begins, more undesirable elements are detected. Back to His table we go for some more treatment. Some of us have been beaten the second time and the third time. Our trial may come in another package with different wrapping this time, but it is essentially the same test we failed to pass the first time.

One Sister who was injured in an accident for the second time wondered what she hadn't gotten out of her spirit the first time. She prayed, "God, whatever You have to do, work me over now. Don't ever let me go through this again."

Horse trainers have a variety of bits they can use, according to the nature and progress of the horse. When a horse is stubborn and rebellious and insists on his own will, they use a bit that nearly tears his mouth when the reins are pulled. After the horse has become submissive and obedient, however, that harsh bit can be replaced by a much gentler one. The horse barely feels its presence in his mouth, yet responds at the slightest touch of the reins.

That's the way God wants us to be. He doesn't enjoy harshness. He has something glorious in store for us. But, if we are unfit for His plan, what choice does He have? In love He must be firm with us. He would prefer gentleness. This process is not as hard as you think. Just surrender. Let Him do His work. It is hard because you are resisting. You are not sure if you want to forsake all, to give Him all, to be fully separated from the world. There were certain elements of the world that you might still love and not want to give up. You are making His work hard. When we jump on God's side with both feet and cease to resist His workings in us, then the blessings come and the unspeakable joys.

There are realms of the Spirit that we will never enter if we insist on taking things of the flesh with us. He won't permit it. We will forever remain on the threshold of greatness if we are determined to hold on to the things of the world. They will not pass through the scrutiny of the anointing of God and into the place of authority in Him.

God is more anxious than we are to get past this beating and sifting process. He has something wonderful in mind for us. He will not prolong this process any longer than necessary. This process is not an end in itself, this is just part of the larger picture. No father ever enjoyed spanking his children. And we are all glad when they reach the maturity that they no longer need it. God will make us into a glorious vessel. Don't lose sight of that fact.

Did you ever notice that God knows where the tender spots are? Just like a chiropractor probing for that sore spot, the Lord finds your "sore spot" and works on it. You cry out in pain. You would prefer that He not deal with that area. But He must! That's where the problem is. Let Him put you back on the table and get you ready for a glorious future as one of His chosen vessels.

"Do I have to go through all this?" you ask.

No, you don't have to. You can be a wallflower if you want to. You can just sit there if you want to. I want to be a vessel of honor, one used by God. We're talking about becoming vessels, vessels of honor for the Master's use. He won't force you to do it; but, it's a privilege you can't afford to miss.

Chapter Seven

The Mixing

For unto us was the gospel preached, as well as unto them: but the word preached did not profit them, not being mixed with faith in them that heard it. (Hebrews 4:2)

After the clay was completely pulverized, I saw the potter take some straw and some water and begin mixing them with the powdery clay. The straw speaks of strength, the water of the Spirit. There are many applications. The Godhead is made up of Father, Son and Holy Ghost. *"For there are three that bear record in heaven, the Father, the Word, and the Holy Ghost: and these three are one. And there are three that bear witness in earth, the spirit, and the water, and the blood: and these three agree in one"* (I John 5:7-8). We are made up of body, soul and spirit. We are a mixture of many ingredients in God.

If we get too much of the Word and not enough of the Spirit, we get lopsided. We need to be balanced Christians. Don't go off on spiritual tangents. Get your feet rooted and grounded in the Word of God. Then, if anything comes along that is contrary to that Word, you will know that it is not of God. And when you do things according to the Word of God, you will find yourself in perfect order, and the blessings of the Lord will rest upon your life.

Without the straw the clay would be weak. Without the water it would have no unity. We need a proper balance.

The potter was very careful not to put too much or too little straw and not to put too much or too little water. If the mixture were too dry, it would not knit together. The water brings unity.

On the other hand, anybody who has mixed concrete knows that if you get too much water with the cement and the sand, you have soup that is impossible to work with. Too much water weakens the mixture as well. Just the right mixture of cement, sand, and water makes a strong bond for any application. When you add the proper amount of stone to the mix, you need a jackhammer to break it up.

If there is too much water in the concrete, it takes too long to set up. With the correct moisture content, it sets up so fast it nearly kills us amateurs finishing it off. You need the right mixture. We need a proper balance of doctrine, a proper balance of experience and a proper balance in the Spirit.

When he was satisfied that the mixture was correct, the potter began to methodically knead the lump of clay. It reminded me of a woman making bread. I didn't fully understand what he was doing. I thought it was just a matter of putting the right things together. It was much more than that. Long after it looked to me as though the clay was well mixed, he continued to work with it. As his hands carefully probed each part of the lump again and again, he was working out the air bubbles. If any air bubbles were left, he told me, the pot would explode when it was placed in the fire and would destroy not only itself, but other vessels that were with it in the oven.

There is a whole lot of hot air (hypocrisy, pride etc.) in some Christians today, and the Holy Ghost is trying to work it out. We don't seem to be bothered. We don't know the dangers. But He is determined to get it out of us. Some are so puffed up. Some walk around with a chip on their shoulder. Do you have any like that in your church?

They just dare you to knock it off. They go to church looking for a fight. They had a plaque in Australia that said, "a chip on the shoulder is a sign there's more wood a little higher up."

The Holy Ghost is bursting many bubbles in this last day. He is showing us that we're not going to get to heaven on our own merits. It's God or nothing. It's the Holy Ghost or nothing. Paul said, *"For I know that in me (that is, in my flesh,) dwelleth no good thing..."* (Romans 7:18). *"Who shall deliver me from the body of this death"* (Romans 7:24)? God is working on the weaknesses of our flesh so that we might become the great vessel He has planned. Does He have to keep kneading those sore spots? Yes! He does! Let Him do His work.

When you begin to think that you are really accomplishing something in God, you're in trouble. Many of us have had the experience of praying for the sick, sometimes in great prayer lines. When eight or ten astounding miracles have taken place, you know that you are anointed. The devil admits it too. He tries to get you to gloat over it. But as soon as you entertain the pride he is pushing you toward, you might as well not pray for the rest of the line. Nothing will happen. The devil has injected that little element of pride. Either rebuke him and his filthy pride or stop praying for the sick. God wants all the glory.

Satan knows how to pull you down. He got pulled down himself. He wants to drag you down with him. That's his job. He thought he could exalt himself against God. He said, *"I will ascend into heaven, I will exalt my throne above the stars of God: I will sit also upon the mount of the congregation, in the sides of the north: I will ascend above the heights of the clouds; I will be like the most High"* (Isaiah 14:13-14). But God said, *"Thou shalt be brought down to hell, to the sides of the pit"* (Isaiah 14:15).

Satan wants you to be lifted up with pride. You must keep your flesh under subjection, as Paul did. When you think you've done something, the Lord will say, "If you think you can do it by yourself, I'll let you do it. I will go help somebody who needs Me. You don't seem to need Me. You think you can do everything by yourself."

We must respond, "Lord, I need You more today than I've ever needed you." We must learn the secret of dependence on God.

One of the major works of the Spirit is to humble us and to exalt Christ. Even the Spirit did not come to *"speak of Himself"* (John 16:13).

In some of my greatest meetings, God has done such great things that it seemed I was watching it all through television. I actually seemed to be only viewing what somebody else was doing. I knew I was there. I knew those were my hands. I knew that was my voice. And yet I knew it wasn't me. I knew it was God. I was just the vessel. I was nearly removed from the situation, because I knew that God was there.

If the Devil can get you to project yourself and make you think you are doing something, you are headed for a fall. If your hands are anointed, if your lips are anointed, if your feet are anointed, make your flesh recognize that anointing. You are only the custodian.

If you were to give me a thousand dollars and say, "Keep this for me," I couldn't go around saying, "Look, this is mine." It would be yours. You were only letting me keep it for you. When I walk into a meeting where I have to minister, I say, "God, if You're not here, and if You don't work, nothing will be done." I am just an instrument that He uses to do His work.

We are guardians of the Holy Ghost anointing. We are permitted to keep it. When the Holy Ghost is ready for it to be used, it begins to flow like a river. We know that God is working, not us.

Let the Holy Ghost burst your bubble. Let Him get all the air out of you. Your flesh won't like it. Flesh wants to be recognized. Some folks get upset if you don't recognize them. When many people are involved in a project and you try to name them publicly, even if you have the best of memories, at some point you will miss somebody. It seems that the one you miss is always the one with the chip on his shoulder.

Many years ago we had only one other family to help us get the camp ready for summer activities. The boys were very young, and because the whole family was short, the boys were very small. It took two or three of them on one end of a box springs or mattress to move it. That made double work on the rest of us. And they kept disappearing. We nearly killed ourselves, going night and day, to get everything done.

One day a newspaper reporter came out from Ashland to do an article on the camp. He took a picture of the boys over by the bell. That picture appeared in the paper with the caption, "Everybody gets Camp ready!" When I saw it, I was so hurt. I wasn't even in the picture. "Everybody?" I said, "I have been running all over the Camp just trying to find those others! Everybody? And my name wasn't even mentioned!" Old flesh wants to be recognized.

An elderly pastor took a young preacher into the mountainous part of Virginia to visit another church. When he saw them enter, the pastor of the church went down to meet them and invited them to sit with him on the platform. "Oh, no, no," the elderly gentleman insisted. "We've just come to get blessed. We'll just sit right here." The young preacher, however, wanted to accept the invitation and be seen on the platform.

"Come on up, the both of you," the host pastor insisted.

"No, we'll just sit right here," the elder answered. But, when he sensed that his young companion wanted to accept, he said to him, "Son, if you want to go up, go ahead. I'll stay here." That was all the young man was waiting for. He gladly went forward.

The service started. The organ and guitars began playing and the people began singing joyfully. After a while, when the service was at fever pitch, the pastor opened a small door under the pulpit, reached into a box, took out a rattlesnake and began to "handle" it. After a little while, he turned and handed the snake to that young preacher, who nearly died with fright.

"Lord," he prayed, "If You will get me out of here alive, I will never be caught in one of these places again!" On the way home, he said to the elder pastor, "Why didn't you tell me?"

"Son," he said, "I did everything I could to keep you from going up there. But I could tell that you really wanted to go. So, I thought, 'Well, if he wants to go, let him go!'" It is important to keep "old flesh" under subjection.

When you want to be seen, the anointing will

subside. If you learn to hide behind the Cross, Jesus will work for you. He said, *"And I if I be lifted up from the earth, will draw all men unto me"* (John 12:32). The higher we lift Him, the more we magnify God, the more God will work for us.

That was the secret of the greatness of Kathryn Kuhlman's ministry. She made you feel that Jesus was sitting right beside you. She made you feel that Jesus was walking with you. She magnified the name of Jesus, and you felt His presence. She knew the secret of exalting Jesus, and that made her a great preacher. When He is lifted up, He works. She became popular as a result of it.

I love the story of David and his three mighty captains. They became great because they made David great. If they had not been willing to get behind the wheel and push David forward, they would never have been great themselves. As David began to gain favor with both God and man, his aids were drawn up with him. Many Christians have to be number one or they don't play. God called us to work with Jesus. He is first, but we always get due recognition—eventually. It may not come when or in the way you expect it, but just be faithful. He never fails.

Many so-called Christians talk like they have the goods. James tells us not to be *"hearers"* of the Word only, but *"doers of the Word"* (James 1:22). Those who are only "hearers" and not "doers" are only deceiving themselves, he said. Don't tell me how many gifts of the Spirit you have received. Let me see them in action. Let the Potter work the hot air out of you.

Chapter Eight

The Molding

*Behold, I am according to thy wish...I also am
formed out of the clay.* (Job 33:6)

When the potter was satisfied that he had all the
bubbles out of the clay, he placed it as a great lump
on the wheel. His wheel was about thirty inches in
diameter and had a pin sticking up in the center—
upon which he placed the clay. With the same stick
he had used to beat the clay, he began to turn the
wheel.

You can't imagine how those hardships and
trials, the circumstances of your life, are working
for you; but they are. Did Saul realize that his

search for his father's lost asses would bring him to the place of anointing? Probably not. He spent three days looking for those animals. He had to walk a long distance, sleep under the stars, and eat the meager provisions he could take along. Even that finally ran out.

Was that the way to get anointed? You probably would have said, "This can't be the way." But your circumstances are tools that God uses to mold and perfect you and to bring you to the place where you can receive a greater anointing and be the vessel God wants you to be.

When Saul had decided to return home without the animals—having run out of food and fearing that his father would be worried that some evil had befallen him—his servant informed him there was a prophet living nearby. When Saul met Samuel, the prophet informed him that he shouldn't worry about his father's animals. They had been found. He wanted Saul to spend the night and he said, *"Tomorrow I...will tell thee all that is in thine heart"* (I Samuel 9:19). The Lord had shown him that Saul was to be *"captain over My people Israel"* (I Samuel 9:16).

In 1960 Dad went to Hagerstown, Maryland, to attend a minister's meeting in Brother Lester Myer's church. He stood up and gave a testimony in that meeting, telling some of the miracles that God had given him in his tent. At the close of the service a man approached him and said, "You're just the man we need in India."

"Did I give a wrong impression?" Dad asked. "I want to make it plain that I don't have a big tent. I have a small tent. Don't think that I'm a big preacher. I don't see how I could go to India."

"Don't worry," the Indian brother said, "My wife has been to America, and she knows how to cook American food. You will be all right with us."

"I wasn't worried about food," Dad said, "I was just thinking that India's a long way away."

"It is a long way," the man said. "But, we need somebody like you in India. We need that faith message. I am praying that God will send you."

That day God put a hook in Dad's spirit, and he didn't rest until he preached in India. He made two trips—in January of 1961, and again a year later. Mother and Ruth (who had been living and ministering in Hong Kong) accompanied him. Ruth stayed in India for three months, and that was the beginning of her world-wide ministry.

When Dad traveled to Hagerstown, he didn't anticipate such wonderful doors opening for him. But, you never know. You will be surprised at the doors that God leads you through. The answer you are looking for may be found right in the midst of your circumstances.

A sister from the eastern shore of Maryland was attending a major crusade in Richmond many years ago. I was invited to say a word in one of the meetings. I announced that a well-known evangelist would be one of our camp speakers that summer and invited everyone to attend. She felt something that made her want to respond. She wanted to get some more of what she felt. She is still coming regularly after many years. You never know where circumstances will take you, who will be there to hear you, whose heart will be touched, and whose life will be changed. The very tool used to do the beating is now used to form the vessel.

The potter spun the wheel with the stick. He turned it faster and faster. Those who work with clay in the Western world have motorized wheels that spin at the push of a button. This potter had to work at it. And whenever the wheel slowed, he would pick up the stick again and use it to get up more speed. I asked him why it had to spin so fast.

"If the wheel is spinning slowly," he answered, "it is very difficult to form the vessel. The faster it spins, the easier my work becomes."

Many people want to do something for God, but they are sitting on a bench doing absolutely nothing.

"What are you waiting for?" I ask them.

"I'm waiting for God," they always say. God can't mold you while you are sitting still. He does it when you get moving.

"I've never been to Bible School."

"I'm afraid!"

"The faster the wheel moves," the potter told me, "the easier it is to form a vessel." You will never get perfected until you get moving. It's easier for God to perfect you while you're moving, while you're doing something, while you're teaching a Sunday School class, while you're visiting a neighbor. It is called "on-the-job training." It's the best kind. It is easier for God to mold us while we are moving than it is when we're motionless.

Have you ever tried to turn the steering wheel of your car when the motor's not running? Try it. On some models, it is nearly impossible. The newer ones will even lock up on you. Then, start the motor, and with one finger you can turn that wheel. If you don't have power steering, let the car drift a little and that steering wheel will begin to move freely.

That's the way it is with our lives in God. Get busy doing something for God. You will make some mistakes. Surely you will. But you will also learn through every mistake. I would rather see a person fail attempting to do something for God than to see that they never attempted anything. Those who never attempted anything for God (and who have succeeded at doing nothing) have no right to criticize those who are attempting to do something. Keep that wheel turning so you can learn more quickly.

The movement makes some uncomfortable. God said through Jeremiah, *"If thou hast run with the footmen, and they have wearied thee, then how canst thou contend with horses..."* (Jeremiah 12:5)? If you can't stand this present movement, what will you do when the flood waters of revival break forth?

Many churches want you to be perfect before they give you an opportunity to do anything. I don't know how they expect you to become perfect. You have to start somewhere. You can't be perfect before you stand and prophesy. You have to start somewhere. If nobody ever gives you the opportunity to preach, how can you grow and develop in God.

In 1970, we took twenty-four people into India. Twelve went north to Chandigar and twelve went with me to Jaipur. Each evening, before the preaching I gave some of the newer ones five or ten minutes to preach through an interpreter. At first they just repeated things that they had been taught and didn't last long. But each evening they got more insight and took longer. After a while, they were doing so well that I wondered if I would get the microphone back. Somebody has to give the young ones an opportunity to start. If not, they never grow and develop.

We take many people with us when we travel in crusades overseas. When hundreds crowd to the altars with many needs, I look to everyone of the team to be able to minister.

Some say, "Brother Heflin, I have never done that before."

"That's okay," I tell them. "Now is a good time to start."

How does a person ever get started in a healing ministry? You have to find the heads of some sick people and lay your hands on them. There is no other way. You just have to start.

How do you get into a prophetic ministry? You find someone that needs to hear from God, and you start prophesying to them. The more you prophesy, the greater your faith becomes. The more you pray for the sick, the more you see God work. At some point, you recognize that while you were busy the Lord has been molding and shaping your life.

How do you learn to lead singing? You have to do it. Perhaps you are afraid to fail. But, what greater failure could there be than to do nothing. The man who buried his talents in the ground for fear of doing something wrong with them or losing them, received the greater judgment. *"I was afraid,"* he said (Matthew 25:30). But, the Lord didn't accept his excuses. He called him an *"unprofitable servant"* and commanded judgment to be served on him. Don't be afraid to make a mistake. Don't bury your talents in fear. Bury your fears instead. Get busy doing something for God.

How do you learn to preach? You have to start preaching. You can never learn if you don't get started. They can't teach these things in Bible School. Dad and I visited a Bible School once. "Everyone who would like to attend the hermaneutics class," we were told, "follow this brother."

I looked at Dad. "What is hermaneutics?" I asked.

"I don't know," he answered.

He had been preaching for forty years and had no idea what the word meant. But, oh could he preach!

Those books don't teach you how to fast and pray and hear the voice of God. They don't teach you how to go to the nations of the world by faith. To learn those things, you have to get up and moving and busy doing something for God. Then He uses you.

The servant of Abraham said, *"...I being in the way, the Lord led me..."* (Genesis 24:27). And while you are busy working for God, enlargement will come. You cannot grow one inch in God while you are sitting on the stool of "do nothing." When you are up and about and busy doing what God has called you to do, great things result.

My father was a country boy who went to Washington, D.C. He had very little formal education. But, at an early age he dedicated himself to the work of the church and he was faithful to that dedication. Before long he had thirteen offices in the church. He said to the pastor, "I'm not sure if I can handle all this. Being Sunday School Superintendent over 1,150 people is beyond my ability. I can't pronounce a lot of the big words they have in the Sunday School quarterly. And I'm not sure I can handle some of those other jobs."

The pastor answered, "Brother Wallace, you're here. You are faithful. You never miss a service. I know that I can depend on you. You will not let me down."

And as my father was busy doing those jobs for God, God was perfecting him into a great faith preacher. Don't just sit waiting for "God's time." Don't wait until something falls from heaven on you. Get busy. Get on God's wheel. Let Him work on you. Your life will be changed.

When an anointed couple from the camp took with them another young lady and were ministering in a Full Gospel Business Men's meeting in Chicago, there were many people who needed to be healed and many who needed to be filled with the Spirit. They wanted to pray for those who needed to be filled with the Spirit. So, the brother said to the people, "I want everyone who is sick to gather over on this side. We have brought a sister with us who has a marvelous healing ministry. She is going to pray for you, and God is going to heal you."

The young sister gulped loudly. But, she thought, "If he said I have a marvelous healing ministry, I must have a marvelous healing ministry." And as she laid hands on the sick, they were healed.

While I was in Brisbane, Australia, many years ago, six hundred people came to a Wednesday night service just after New Year's. After the preliminaries the pastor said to the people, "Brother Heflin has a wonderful prophetic ministry. Don't go home before getting prayed for." And he had to slip out to a special board meeting.

Those people were very obedient to their pastor. Every one of them went forward for prayer. After I prayed and prophesied over one row, they moved back and another row moved forward expectantly. After I had prayed for a while, I noticed that my companion wasn't doing anything. "Brother," I said to him, "if you don't get busy and help me, we'll be here all night." He had never prophesied before.

He placed his hand on a woman's head and did some serious praying. While he was praying, he began to have a vision. He started describing his vision. While he was describing the vision, he heard the lady began to sob. Then he had another vision and prophesied by that vision. We left there about one in the morning.

You have to start somewhere. Every time you have an opportunity jump up and testify. That is a good way to start. Take advantage of your opportunities. That is all that God can expect of you.

When I was very young in the ministry, I had a great desire to begin traveling for God. One day a prophetic word was given over me. The Lord said, "You will go, go, go, go, go, go, go, go, go and wonder if you will ever stop." And it happened. I got to the place that I wondered, "Lord, will you ever let me slow down? Will I ever be able to unpack my suitcase and stay home for a while?"

Then, one year while I was in Jerusalem, the Lord spoke to me saying, "Take your traveling shoes off." That was one of the most difficult years I ever spent. I was accustomed to traveling, but He wanted me to be home to strengthen the work.

Every time the wheel slowed down, the potter got the stick and began twirling it again until he was satisfied with the speed. As the wheel spun, I saw the potter plunge his thumbs deep into the top of the clay. With his thumbs he began to form the inside of the vessel and with his other fingers he formed the outside of the vessel. Within seconds he had formed a beautiful vessel, then another and another.

When God created the world and everything in it, He used only His word. He spoke and it was. But when He made man, He used His hands to form man of the dust of the earth. He is still shaping us by hand. It was the pressure of the potter's hands, forcing his thumbs downward, that made the opening and began to form the vessel. The hands of God are upon your soul to mold and perfect you, to make of you the vessel that God wants you to be.

Don't blame the devil for everything. That poor fellow gets blamed for so much that he has nothing to do with. In our ignorance, we blame him for the pressures we undergo, when all the time we're under the pressure of the hands of God. Recognize the dealings of the Holy Ghost. He is molding us and perfecting us. He is making of us a vessel. You cannot be formed properly without the gentle pressure of the Potter's hands. And the more pressure He puts on us the faster we can be formed.

The devil tempts you—trying to make you fall. God tests you—trying to make you strong. Let's recognize the difference and yield ourselves to the workings of God. For He says, *"...the trying of your faith worketh patience. But let patience have her perfect work, that ye may be perfect and entire, wanting nothing"* (James 1:3-4).

Some pastors don't dare let God apply pressure through their sermons. They might lose some offerings. So, they preach "wonderful" sermons, but lives are not molded. "Be kind to your neighbor." "Contribute to the United Way Campaign." "Give old clothes to the street people. Be concerned and say a prayer for those in need." Etc. etc. You will never get molded on that diet. Pressure is required.

Sometimes the Holy Ghost tightens the screws on us so much that we feel that we are in a vise. He turns up the heat so much we are sure we are in a pressure cooker. Sometimes the pressure makes us feel uncomfortable and we become irritable with those around us, thinking that they are annoying us. But, thank God, something is happening. We are growing in God. Our weaknesses are being converted into strengths. Don't despise the pressure; and don't take out your frustrations on someone nearby.

Sometimes He is working us over so strongly at the altar that we feel like lying down and dying. "You are killing me, Lord," we say. Good! That's what He wants to do. The sooner you get "killed" the sooner God can do something beautiful through you. When you get up from there, you will know that He has done His work.

I asked the potter another interesting question: "Are you ever unable to make the vessel that you had in your mind to make?"

"No," he answered. "But, at times I am unable

to perfect a vessel as I would wish. The clay has a will of its own.''

"You mean that dirty clay over there has a will of it's own?" I asked incredulously.

"Yes, it has a will of its own," he said. "It resists my hands and resists the pressure I am putting on it. I can still form something. But, I am unable to perfect that vessel to the degree I desire.''

Is it not true of your soul and mine? There are things that God wants to do with our lives that we won't let Him do. We put up a barrier and say, "God, this far and no farther. Don't touch this particular area. Leave it as it is.'' God may desire to do something wonderful in us, but if He is resisted by our own will, He cannot make us into the vessel He desires. Allow your will to be brought under subjection to the will of God, so that His perfect plan for you can be accomplished. Parts of us may be beautifully formed, while other parts remain ugly and deformed because our own self-will, our flesh doesn't permit a perfect work to be done.

Is it an indictment of God because a vessel is flawed? No! It is an indictment against the vessel itself which has resisted God's dealing. If people would only stop looking at Christians and look at Christ! He never fails.

Even Jesus had to bring His own will into subjection to His Father's will. He said, "...*not My* will, but Thine, be done'' (Luke 22:42). He agonized over that decision. You must have, somewhere, sometime, that same Gethsemane experience. You must agonize before God until you become willing to sell out completely to Him. When you do, you will be ready for the Master's touch. He wouldn't come down from the cross when they taunted Him. He had made His decision.

When you make the same commitment, "not my will but Thine," you will no longer respond to God with "it is too early in the morning;" "it is too late at night;" "it is too far;" "it is too hot;" "it is too cold." You will be ready to comply with anything God requires of you.

You are your own worst enemy. If you can get victory over your own flesh, you won't have difficulty conquering all your other lesser enemies. Once, while teaching in Australia, Mother said, "I see you brought your greatest enemy with you to church this morning.''

I spoke up and said, "Yes, that devil follows me wherever I go.''

"Son," she answered, "the devil is not your greatest enemy.''

She was right. I am my own worst enemy. You are your own worst enemy. You have a will of your own.

Once I prophesied over a young man of great promise. God said to him, "If you want to be average, you can be average. If you want to be mediocre, you can be mediocre. But if you want to be great, I will make you great." I am sad to say that young man settled for second best. Your will determines God's limits.

People come to me and say, "Brother Heflin, I don't understand why God's not doing more with me. I don't know what's standing in the way!" I usually don't believe them. Most of us know exactly what the problem is, exactly what is preventing us from moving on and doing more for God. If we would be honest, we would all say, "I know exactly what has been the hindrance to my receiving the greater thing that God wants me to have." If we could just yield our whole will to Him, we would see greater things done for God.

Many times we are comfortable where we are and resist further change. We don't want to submit to the greater pressure necessary to form us into that more glorious vessel. Thank God He hasn't given up on us.

The measure of a man or woman of God is not intellect, ability or appearance or even attainment, but the willingness to grow into the place spiritually that he/she can handle the vision and the revelation that God desires to give.

Works all over America have folded. Somebody heard from God. God gave them something to do. They started well, but later folded. Many imagine that the original vision was not from God. "If it was of God, it would have continued," they say.

No! I believe it was of God. The problem was not with God or the vision. The problem is that we have to keep growing in God to be able to handle the ever-unfolding vision. And it is not all spiritual. We must be able to handle the vision physically, as well as spiritually. Get your own flesh out of the way to make room for all that God desires to do, or it will all come to naught.

There is a great responsibility on every one of us. We try to blame God. It is not His fault. It is ours. When we become willing for God to do things as He wills, then He is perfectly able to do all that He has promised. God is looking for men and women upon whom He can pour responsibility.

Some factory workers make good money. But the supervisor or foreman always makes better money. He or she can do your job and many more, but also has the ability to get others working. It is the same in God. The more things you are willing to learn to do in the Spirit, the more capable you become in God, the more valuable you become to Him. He is looking for men and women whom He can trust because the kingdom of God is about to explode with growth.

Willingness is a problem in the church through-out the world. One pastor said he had a willing church. "Ten per cent are willing to serve the

Lord," he said, "and the other ninety per cent are willing to let them do it." Most people never do anything for God because they are unwilling to start with small things. Don't worry! If you are faithful in the small things, God has promised to give you the larger things to do.

When I was in India in 1970, I met an ex-government official who had left his well-paying position to serve God. If you have an official position in India, you have something very important. He was within several years of retirement, and if he left his job and went to work in "the Faith Home," he would begin where everyone else had begun—cleaning the toilets. Many others had preceded him and had become great men and women of God. He made his decision to serve God.

Many would like to be president of the firm before they learn how to run the elevator. Some want to stand behind the pulpit and tell everyone else how to live before they have lived it themselves. Get willing to be what God wants you to be. Just get your will in line with God's will. Let him form you into the vessel He has in mind. He knows what He is doing.

As I watched in amazement, very quickly the vessels began to take form. It almost looked easy. There were large ones and small ones. The Bible says, *"In a great house there are not only vessels of gold and of silver, but also of wood and of earth;*

and some to honour, and some to dishonour" (II
Timothy 2:20), and tells us not to ask the Potter,
"Why hast Thou made me thus" (Romans 9:20)? It
is His choosing. He knows what He is doing.

The potter made at least seven types of vessels,
of varying shapes and sizes. There were tall vessels,
short vessels and medium-size vessels. They were
for every conceivable use. Some vessels just sit on
a shelf holding flowers. They are beautiful. Others
are used for very different purposes. Does the
vessel know what is best? No, but the one forming
it knows. Some of the tiniest vessels hold the most
costly commodities, for instance French perfume.
It is very valuable. It only comes in a small bottle.

Why did God make you a small vessel? He has
something very precious to put inside of you. We
don't have to worry if we're the large economy
size, the medium size, or even if we're the small
size. There is a special purpose for every one of us.
Are you just a water glass? That glass is valuable.
What people wouldn't give sometimes for a glass of
cool water!

One mother's day, I went to the florist to buy
some flowers for my mother. I saw a tiny vase with
only three long-stemmed red roses in it. It was so
petite, so lovely.

"May I help you," the lady asked.

"I want that one for my mother," I answered.

If they had put those three long-stemmed, red roses in some large gaudy vase, they would have detracted from the beauty of the contents. That was just the right vessel for just the right use. Florists are getting smart. They know that the container is just as important as the flowers it holds. And God thinks we are important containers. He made us for a special use.

Don't let the devil torment you with the fact that you are small and insignificant. Say to him, "I might be small, but I house precious things! The anointing of the Holy Ghost resides in and flows out of me!"

"You don't hold much," he'll say.

"No! Neither does that perfume bottle. But, what it does hold is so powerful that just a small drop fills an entire house with fragrance. The fragrance of God's touch flows from my soul. God made me this way—on purpose."

Several years ago, when one of the elderly sisters in our congregation was very ill, God spoke that He was not taking her home because she was such a prayer warrior. At the same time, that sister was undergoing a severe attack by the enemy. "What are you good for?" he asked her. "What are you doing for God? You're old. You're sickly. You have been spending so much time in the hospital. What can you do for God? You are incapable of doing any real work. All you can do is pray.''

When she recovered enough to get back into church, someone told her what God had said about her. Her soul was set on fire to know that God had seen purpose in her life.

There are many people who cannot travel to other countries for the Lord. They cannot go up and down the street knocking on doors to witness. Are they valuable? They certainly are.

From the same lump that produced those giant vessels, God has made you and me. Hallelujah! He has a work for every one of us to do, and what He has called you to do is just as important as that of the great vessels He has formed. They are from the same lump and are fashioned by the same hands.

Just let Him use you. Shine wherever you are. Sparkle for God. You will see that men and women around you admire the anointing and glory that is upon your soul.

Some vessels are so versatile they can be used for many things. I believe that is what God wants of us. He may use us one moment in one way, the next moment in another, totally different way. We must be willing to be what He wants us to be. And why should we fight that? Variety is the spice of life. God wants to give us some new experiences, some new opportunities, and some new thrills.

Just to know that "*...we have this treasure in*

earthen vessels..." is a wonderful miracle (II Corinthians 4:7). His power and anointing is within us. And we are signs of His purchase.

In Jeremiah 32, the prophet's nephew visited him in prison and asked him to buy a piece of land he owned in Benjamin. God had told Jeremiah that houses and fields and vineyards would be returned to His people and to useful production, and he believed God (verse 15). So, the purchase was made and the proper documents of purchase were drawn up. When they were properly signed and sealed they were placed in an earthen vessel until God would redeem His people from their enemies(verse 14).

We are the earthen vessels that hold the evidence of God's purchase. I prefer this privilege to being a millionaire. A millionaire can lose his money in the stock market. The glory and anointing which God has placed in these earthen vessels is the most precious thing we could ever possess.

Let Him make of you what He will.

Chapter Nine

The Sprinkling

And Moses took of the anointing oil...and sprinkled it upon Aaron...and upon his sons....
                                        (Leviticus 8:30)

Moreover he sprinkled with blood both the tabernacle, and all the vessels of the ministry.
                                        (Hebrews 9:21)

As the potter worked with the clay, he continually dipped his hands in water and sprinkled the lump. He would fashion a little, then sprinkle more water on the lump. The movement of air about the spinning clay dried it out. If the clay became dry, it created friction against the potter's hands and prevented him from fashioning it. A constantly fresh anointing is essential to the fashioning process.

This is the daily refilling of the Spirit. Water is a type of the Spirit of God. How often do you need to be refilled with the Spirit? Doing it every day won't hurt you. Many don't even know that they can be refilled.

The disciples of Jesus were filled with the Holy Ghost on the Day of Pentecost. Several days later the book of Acts records a prayer meeting in which the place where they were assembled was shaken and *"they were all filled with the Holy Ghost..."* (Acts 4:31). They had just been baptized in the Spirit a few days before. But, they had come to realize that they needed to be refilled again and again and again. The more we are refreshed in the Spirit, the easier it is for God to change us. If you resist these refillings, you will experience a dry period in which things will not go well for you.

The moistening not only makes the clay pliable, but causes it to glide under the potter's touch. The movement of the potter's hands, the pressure he applies would cause friction, chafing and irritation if the moisture content were not correct. You cannot afford to get dried out even for a moment. You cannot become hard. Those who are dry in their spirits are unresponsive to the Word. You have to first get them to enter into the Spirit through praise and to open up to God before anything can be done for them.

When the glory is falling on us, we'll do anything for the Lord. That's why He continually dips His hand in the water and refreshes us in the Holy Ghost. Without the moving of the Spirit the Word becomes hard, dogmatic and legalistic. If you just keep cutting people with the Word, that gets old. That blade gets dull after a while and bruises. You do great harm. Let the Spirit move as He wills to prepare hearts for change.

You can't change yourself. We are changed by God *"from glory to glory"* (II Corinthians 3:18). That's why the devil doesn't want us to live in the glory. He doesn't want glory to descend in our gatherings. He knows that if there is no glory there is no change. When the glory comes down, God changes us and brings us closer to His likeness and image. We take a new step in Him.

Let the refreshing come! Let that anointing come! Don't let the enemy cause a dryness in your soul. Let the cool, refreshing of the Holy Ghost come. With that anointing upon us, He can further fashion us quickly and take us into new realms.

When a pipe fitter wants to cut a piece of galvanized pipe, he uses a sharp blade. But, if he fails to apply some cutting oil, he won't get very far. Before long so much friction builds up that the pipe begins to smoke. The blades burn up and are quickly worn out. He must stop every few minutes and apply more oil.

It's the same thing in the Spirit. That's why we attend church services and shout and dance and worship God. In order to withstand the pressure that God is putting on us, we need a constantly fresh anointing. We can't dry out.

I am a Pentecostal and am proud of it. But, I am sad that in Pentecostal churches too many times the pastors are using the Word as a hammer with which to beat the sheep over the head.

"Don't do this! Don't do that! Don't do the other thing! You can't do this! You can't do that. You had better not do this! You had better not do that!"

The poor people, who sit there and constantly hear "don't" and "can't" and "you had better not," sink lower and lower in their seats, until finally their spirit is broken. They no longer have joy. They no longer have liberty.

Why don't those preachers who are constantly telling us what we "can't" do start telling us what we can do? We can shout and dance and praise the Lord. That will prepare us to stand against all the legitimate "do not's" of the faith and be victorious. That negative approach just brings people into bondage.

I don't do many worldly things, not because the church says I shouldn't do them, but because I don't want to do them. I want to keep this anointing! I want to keep this joy! I want to keep this freedom! I want to continue feeling what I'm feeling! I know that, if I go backward and do those worldly things, I would lose what God has given me.

If someone told you that you were going to give a thousand dollars to God, you might think they were the biggest liar going. But, when you go to an anointed service where God is moving, you may well be moved to give that money. And you will. Why? Not because someone said you had to, but because you don't want to lose that anointing you feel. You don't want to lose that sweet fellowship. You want to obey God. You want to please Him. You want to show Him your love. Nobody is forcing you to do it, but you do it because you want to.

"...so let him give; not grudgingly, or of necessity: for God loveth a cheerful giver" (II Corinthians 9:7). The anointing makes it easy. You need a constantly fresh anointing. If it is not there, God cannot work on shaping you as He wills.

When you are in a situation that prevents you from getting to church as much as you need to, or the church you are attending is dry, it hurts when God works on you. You feel sometimes, "If I don't get to a place where I can take a fresh drink and get a fresh sprinkling of the Holy Ghost on my soul,

I'm going to die!'' Go where the saints are shouting the victory! Go where the anointing is flowing. Get that continual refreshing and sprinkling of the Spirit.

In India, it is a common practice to keep a water vessel outside the house. Many times a day someone pours water on the outside of that vessel to keep it moist. If they are faithful to do that, the water inside remains cool and refreshing. If not, it gets overheated and becomes unfit for drinking. Keep your spirit fresh. Don't let it get stagnant. Even oil will spoil if it is left unmoved for long periods. You have to stir it up. Take some out. Put new oil in. A lot of saints haven't had a refilling in twenty-five years. Get stirred. Get some new oil.

When the potter moistened the clay, it became slick under his hands, and in no time at all a beautiful vessel was formed. God is working within every one of us. None of us will ever be the same. Let His hand fashion you.

Chapter Ten

The Separation

I drew them with cords of a man, with bands of love: and I was to them as they that take off the yoke on their jaws, and I laid meat unto them.
(Hosea 11:4)

When the potter finished fashioning that vessel, he picked up a piece of string, eighteen inches to two feet long, dipped it in water, wrapped it around the bottom of the vessel and, with a quick movement, separated it from the rest of the lump and set it aside to dry. It happened so quickly. One moment that vessel was still part of the lump. The next moment it was able to stand on its own.

I asked the Lord, "What does that mean to us spiritually?"

God said, "The string represents those 'cords' those 'bands of love' spoken of in My Word. I separate you with cords of love."

I am not talking about being separated from the presence of God. Never! Without Him you are nothing.

I am not talking about discontinuing fellowship with your brothers. You need it, and you will always need it. When you get to be a great man or woman of God, you will still need a spiritual friend to whom you can say, "I need your spiritual advice," and can know that they will tell you what "thus saith the Lord." Many people will give you advice according to what they know you want to hear. Find somebody who will be honest with you and tell it "like it is." If you need to be patted on the back, they will pat you on the back; and if you need to be kicked in the seat, they will do it. It will do you good.

In 1976, the World Pentecostal Conference was held in London. I did everything possible to get a well-known American evangelist to accompany our group that was attending.

"I'm too busy," he told me. "I can't go."

The second or third night of the conference he walked in. I couldn't believe it. "Where did you come from," I asked him?

"I need to talk to you," he said.

When the service had finished, I took our tour group back to the hotel, and we got in a taxi and started riding through the streets of London, trying to find a restaurant that was open. When we found one, we sat together for the next two hours and talked.

"I'm here because I need some advice," he said. "I'm at a crossroads. I feel that you will give me counsel according to the Word of God, without pulling any punches. I flew three thousand, three hundred miles to get it."

Did that make me think any less of my friend? No! It made me feel that he was even a greater man than I had previously thought. He didn't want to make a mistake. He didn't want to have regrets down the road. He was willing to go so far, at such expense, in order to find out what God wanted. Each of us need a friend who can give us godly counsel. That will keep us from falling into many problems.

Some years back when the shepherding and discipleship doctrines were playing havoc with the saints of God in America and many other parts of the world, I was speaking about it, in a Nairobi Hotel, with the founder of a large Christian business men's movement and two well known missionaries to Africa.

"The reason it became so strong," said one of the

missionaries "is that all of us failed to raise our voices, thinking that those who propagated these doctrines had to be right because of who they were. Because we were silent, they felt they had no one to turn to for spiritual counsel. And much harm was done to the Body of Christ as a result."

We need to hear from God through our faithful brothers and sisters. Don't be a loner. Find someone who can give you direction. If not, your life will be completely ruined.

By "separation from the lump" I mean being able to stand on your own two feet. That certainly doesn't mean that God is finished with you. But, you have reached a new stage. That vessel had a certain lovely form, but was not yet of any use until it could stand alone. It was still attached to the unformed lump.

When a child is born, the umbilical cord is cut. For nine months it has taken nourishment from its mother, and she has eaten for two. Now, it is a separate individual. The chord must be cut.

Two matching vessels are lovely together, but you need to make up your mind. If your husband isn't willing to go on with God, you stand on your own. If your wife isn't willing to make a deeper commitment, you stand on your own. If your brothers or sisters have reached a certain level in God and have no hunger to go deeper, you must stand on your own and continue on to the level that God wants you to have.

When I got saved, that made four preachers in our family. But, I couldn't live off my dad's experience. I couldn't live off my sister's experience. I had to stand on my own. I had to move in for myself. I couldn't wait for a family fast day. I had to feel the drive of the Holy Spirit in my own soul, compelling me to fast and separate myself in order to come into the depth and anointing God had for me.

Sometimes, the devil makes you feel that God has thrown you overboard. He sent you to Haiti by yourself. You are separated from the rest of the lump. But, He hasn't cast you aside. With cords of love He separates you and makes you a unique vessel for a unique purpose. He sends you to do a particular job for the glory of God. He separates you to go to Bible School. He separates you for the mission field. He separates you for some other field of service. It isn't easy to leave those we love more than the members of our own family. But, when God puts His hand on us, we must recognize the day of separation and launch out into the ministry He has called us to.

It is just as important to know when to get separated as it is to know when not to get separated. The "wait's" of God and the "stop's" of God are just as important as the "go's" of God. Some people try to separate a vessel that is not ready for separation. The unprepared believers get off by themselves, and the devil starts shooting at them.

Some people think that they are God's gift to creation. No one can tell them anything. Their pastor can't tell them anything. They are determined to stand alone, despite all the advice to the contrary. Sometimes you just have to let them do their own thing. They have to learn the hard way. Don't worry, in God's time there will be an open door for you. God will have someone to listen to you. The Word says, *"A man's gift maketh room for him, and bringeth him before great men"* (Proverbs 18:16).

I hadn't been saved very long when someone called me on the phone and worked me over for a solid hour. "You're tied to your mother's apron stings," they said. "Why don't you get away from your mother and dad. Step out and do something on your own for God. Join our organization. If you don't, you'll never have open doors for your ministry. When you do get souls saved, you'll have nowhere to send them!"

But, I knew I wasn't ready to get out on my own. I knew it wasn't the right time yet. God had me right where He wanted me, and I held steady. The very next day I got a letter from the Philippines inviting me to come and preach. I had just been told the day before that I would never have any opportunities to preach, no open doors, if I stayed

with my parents ministry. The devil wants you to
be separated before you are fully formed. If you
wait on God's timing, the world opens to you. If
you rush ahead of him, you stay a long time,
ministering in your own little sand box.

Then, in 1970, I traveled for nine months
overseas alone. It was very difficult. If you don't
believe me, try it sometime. It was difficult to
leave home for such a long time. It wasn't easy to
be away from my family and the church. But, God
pulled the string. He did the separating. God had
great wisdom when He sent the disciples out two
by two. But, each one must be able to stand alone.

Many people try to get you out there on your
own too soon or they go out alone themselves
before they are ready. Their strength is in the
lump. They need to remain there longer and be
sustained. Don't run ahead of God. We had a very
tragic example at the camp many years ago:

We took a young man off the streets of Richmond. He was just a wanderer. He'd get a job and
work two or three weeks until he had some
money, then lay off for a couple of months and do
nothing. He began to drop by the church, so we
took him out to the camp to give him time to
change. And he got saved.

During camptime that year, we let him testify
in the young people's service in the "Little Tabernacle." Surprisingly, he did a wonderful job. You

wouldn't want to listen to him every day, but considering where he came from and what God had done for him, it was a joy to listen to his testimony.

Light and darkness are so far removed. He had come a long way. Many were moved by the amazing change that God had brought about in him; and when an offering was taken for him, they gave. The offering amounted to ten or fifteen dollars, which in those days was wonderful.

But, the most important part of the story is that everyone walked past and told the brother how much they had been blessed by his testimony, how they appreciated him. Well, that turned out to be the worst thing that could have happened to that young man. He was convinced that he was a full-fledged evangelist and soon left for Florida to preach. But, he wasn't strong enough to survive and only created problems in Florida.

Standing to give a fifteen minute testimony doesn't make you an evangelist. In fifteen minutes, he had told his entire experience with God. That was all he had. Once he gave his testimony, he didn't have anything else to give. The seed, the Word of God, hadn't gotten its roots down deep enough in him. He separated himself from the lump in pride, thinking that he was ready to stand on his own. He thought he could continue to "bless the socks off of people" and that the world would come beating a path to his door. He was wrong. His message could be compared to Beech Nut baby food or Pablum. He wasn't ready to be separated.

Let the Lord do the separating. Stay with the lump until He cuts you loose. You don't know the proper timing. He does! Let Him show you the proper timing. Don't be too anxious to get out on your own.

Many people, from all over the world, are blessed to live here at our camp and get training and preparation for the work of God. Those who do well go out to the nations of the world, traveling for God. While they are here, they don't have the pressures of a monthly house payment, a monthly car payment, and daily provisions for their families and themselves. It is easier to yield yourself to God without all those pressures on you.

A salesman who doesn't "have to" sell does better than one who "has to." The pressure is off. He is more relaxed and doesn't have to pressure his clients. We all resent strong sales pressure. At times we're almost afraid to look at an item for fear of being pressured to buy. The first lesson we learned in selling was, "Everyone wants 'the privilege' of buying." We were taught to ask questions like: "Would you like your payment on the first or the fifteenth?" "Do you like the blue one or the red one?" "Do you want it delivered on Wednesday or Friday?"

They haven't even said they want it yet. But, you assume they are buying because you give them that privilege. "Do you want it?" is a question you never ask. You assume they want it. When you start putting pressure on them, they start to back off. They have a car payment due. They have a home mortgage note due.

It's the same in the Spirit. If you feel too pressured, you're not at your best. So, we have felt led to relieve those who are preparing to work for God from those daily pressures.

Recently, I advised an enthusiastic young person not to quit his job just yet to dedicate himself to full-time service. That may surprise some, because we certainly encourage people to live by faith. But, the timing is important. Many quit their jobs before they are fully prepared to serve the Lord and bring severe hardships on themselves. Youthful zeal always wants to do it all now. But, God has a perfect timing. If you quit your job before your ability to preach and minister can sustain you, you're in trouble. Leave your other job when your ministry can support you.

Just because you love God and can say "hallelujah" is not a sign that you are ready to be separated from the lump. Stay on the job. Keep praying. Keep fasting. Get yourself into the place where the Holy Ghost can move in and through you. Take advantage of every opportunity to grow spiritually. Before you know it, the separation will come; and you'll leave that job and go full-time for God!

Sometimes it has been a blessing to us to have only a limited number of our camp buildings winterized. If we had unlimited space, we would be overrun with people leaving their jobs and looking for a place to stay. The purpose of the camp training is for people who have a mature sense of what God is doing in them and a desire to get out and do something for God. Those who are serious about God's call are soon separated for service.

While it is true that we must not run ahead of God, we must also guard against minimizing what God is doing in us. It doesn't take God fifteen years to get you ready. He will do it at your own pace. It can happen very quickly, more quickly than you imagine. At the marriage in Cana in Galilee, when Mary told Jesus that the wine had run out—expecting Him to do something about it—He answered her, *"Woman, what have I to do with thee? Mine hour is not yet come"* (John 2:4).

Mary didn't answer Him. She knew what the angel Gabriel had said to her. She knew what God had spoken through Elizabeth in prophecy. She remembered the words of Simeon, when his eyes had fallen on the Redeemer in the Temple that day. She turned to the servants and said, *"Whatsoever He saith unto you, do it"* (verse 5) and walked away.

Jesus saw some stone waterpots sitting there and said, *"Fill the waterpots with water"* (verse 7). When they had obeyed the first command, He said *"Draw out now, and bear unto the governor of the feast..."* (verse 8). They obeyed and witnessed a miracle. But, it wasn't wine until they started to pour it out. If they had allowed it to remain in the jugs, it would have remained water. When they started to pour, it became wine. Start pouring out. God will do the miracle. The need will be met.

Mary's faith in the Word, spoken to her by angels and through prophets, caused the ministry of Jesus to begin before it might have otherwise. Spiritual leaders may see more in you than you can see in yourself. They have a greater vision of what God is going to do with you and, hopefully, they will encourage you. Most pastors won't purposely hold you back. They must give an account to God for their care of your soul. Most will do it with great care.

Some people want to stay in school all their lives. They are never ready. They always feel they lack something. They are professional students. They feel safe. They don't have to face the real world. They get one grant after another to study. They are afraid to be separated for their life's work. We need to help them get started.

Paul said to Timothy, *"...stir up the gift of God, which is in thee..."* (II Timothy 1:6). That gift was already in him. He got it through the laying on of hands. He just needed to stir it up. When you receive the Holy Ghost, you receive the nine gifts of the Spirit. They are in you. The Holy Ghost can prophesy. He can heal the sick. He can do miracles. Those gifts are in you. You just need to stir them up. Someone must encourage you to do it and allow you to do it.

A family came from Australia to attend camp-meeting. The husband's parents were old-fashioned Pentecostal believers, and his brother was a Pentecostal preacher. I assumed that he had preached some himself. So, one day I announced that he would be the speaker in the afternoon service. His message lasted only about twenty minutes. Then, I felt led to call everyone to the front and challenge the brother to lay hands on them and prophesy.

I later learned that he had neither preached nor prophesied before. But, he leaned across the pulpit and prayed for God to help him. I led him down front and placed my hand on his back and he gave a short word over six or seven people. I knew most of the people and knew that his word was "right on." One woman got so excited.

"Brother Heflin," she said breathlessly, "did you hear what he said? Did you hear?" Then, she looked at me strangely and said, "You didn't tell him anything about me, did you?"

"Yes!" I said jokingly. "He is staying in my house. I kept him up all night long and told him about everyone who is attending camp. And he has the best memory I have ever seen."

Several days later I felt led to announce that the wife would be speaking in the afternoon service. She later testified, "When he made that announcement, I went to the house, threw myself across the bed and cried for two hours. If I had known how to get to the airport, I would have left this country so fast. Brother Heflin didn't know it, but I have been the worst introvert. I couldn't go outside my house when my neighbor was in the yard. I didn't want to talk to anybody."

But she got up that day and spoke for forty minutes. When she finished, I called everyone to the front to be prophesied over. She was so frightened that she closed her eyes tightly and didn't open them until she had prophesied over everyone. She prophesied over her own two teenaged daughters, without ever knowing that she had laid hands on them.

When it was time for the children to return to school, she took them home, but the husband accompanied me to Mombasa, Kenya and was the best preacher I had. When he returned home, he became his brother's assistant. His wife became head of Women's Aglow for the entire country and went to Canada to represent the movement. She began prophesying by vision. Many preachers later told me that they hadn't taken the camp ministry seriously—until they saw the amazing changes in that couple.

Someone has to give young ones an opportunity. As we encourage others, we grow ourselves. Most of the people that we train and send overseas—and who do a fantastic work for God—would not qualify as missionaries with most organizations.

One brother has two master's degrees, and his wife is very well educated also. They have ministered now throughout the world with great success for twenty years. But, they would have been disqualified by most because they had four children. Most organizations want candidates who are neither too old or too young (they consider twenty-five to thirty-five to be the optimum age), married (for stability), but with no more than two children, college graduates (preferably with graduate degrees in at least two fields), with theological training and with several years of experience. If you fall anywhere outside these qualifications, you are not considered. That eliminates many people who want to work for God.

Then, you must attend language school and take cultural training. By that time most people have lost the vision and the anointing. I would much rather have a zealous few anointed by the Spirit. They get more done.

Most of the people who travel with us would be considered by most groups, at first, to be unqualified. Later, when they have fasted and prayed and gotten themselves into a place of anointing in God, and when others begin to see what God is doing in them, everybody wants them. They are willing to sleep on the floor or make whatever other sacrifice necessary to do God's work. They have gone through a rigorous on-the-job training. They are ready to do fantastic things for God, because someone believed in them. We must encourage one another. We all need it at some point.

If we send people who are not able to stand on their own, we send them with someone more experienced who can stand. If they had been sent alone, they would not have known where to go and what to do. Not knowing anyone in the first country they entered they would have checked into a hotel, quickly spent all their money, become discouraged by persecutions and the difficulty of getting open doors, and would have called home to say they were returning on the next flight. So, we send a weak one with a strong one. If one stumbles and falls, the other is there to pick them up.

The day we licensed a sister, who has been with us for many years, God spoke to her in prophecy and said, "You have gone with others. From now on others will go with you; for I have caused you to grow in the Spirit. You will stand, and it will be your wisdom and your insight that bring the victory and the deliverance." Her time of separation had come.

I have counseled people not to go overseas by themselves. I could sense that they weren't ready. But, I couldn't convince them. They were so determined to make it on their own they wouldn't listen. They stumbled and fell because they didn't know what to do.

When you are in a strange country where you don't know anyone, you don't know the language, you have no open doors to minister, you have to know God and know that He sent you. You must have your feet rooted and grounded in God. He opens doors and makes a way for you. Wait for the separation.

There are ministries that want to hold on to you. You may come up under them or are associated with them, or perhaps they trained you and prepared you, and they want to hold on to you and not let you go. Whatever you do or say they will try to make you feel that you cannot survive without them. They have a strangle hold on you.

We take just the opposite attitude. I want to let people go—when they are ready. I want to let them go. If we err, it is on the side of encouraging people to get out and work for God. I'm not saying I want to get rid of them. No! I need more help in the ministry. But, I want that individual to get to the place they can stand on their own two feet. And because we are willing to encourage them, because we say to them, "Come on, you can do it! Get out there! Come on! You can make it!" there is a greater bond of fellowship between us.

Now when they need me, I know it's not because I told them they needed me. It's because they have gotten out there themselves and found out it's a hard, cruel world; and we need fellowship and unity of spirit to survive. The ties between us are stronger than ever—as a result of our being willing to release them.

Our people who travel write us and keep us posted on what is happening overseas. They are largely on their own, yet they feel the strength of this tie. They need us. We need them. We pray for them every day. They pray for us every day. When they need our help, in some more concrete form, they know that they can pick up the phone and call us, and we'll believe God together for an answer. Something will be done. God will make a way.

Paul and Barnabas did a wonderful work in Antioch. But the day came when God had a greater work for them to do. One day God spoke to the leaders there, *"Separate Me Barnabas and Saul for the work whereunto I have called them"* (Acts 13:2). They obeyed, even though it would mean loss for them. *"And when they had fasted and prayed, and laid their hands on them, they sent them away"* (verse 3).

Philip was a faithful deacon, but one day God spoke to him to be separated from the church at Jerusalem and sent him to bring revival to Samaria.

God doesn't thrust us out (separate us) brusquely. He does it tenderly, yet decisively. If you continue to be hardheaded and stubborn, He might do like the mother eagle does. Under the straw in the nest she puts thorns. Then, when it is time for the eaglets to soar on their own, she begins to remove the soft portions of the nest, leaving the exposed sharp points to torment the young ones. When the thorns have pricked you long enough, you may decide you want to learn to fly. You may decide it is time to get out and obey God. You will eventually get tired of sitting on those thorns! It's time for the separation from the nest.

Oh, don't worry. When the little eaglet tries to fly for the first time and fails, the mother swoops down and catches him on her back and carries him again to the heights. Each time the eaglet does a little better, until finally his wings are strong enough and have caught the stride; and he is able to soar off by himself. What must it look like to that tiny eaglet falling though space? It must seem that the ground is coming up very fast. But, as long as he needs her, his mother is there. Be there for

people who need you. Don't leave them, until they
can fly alone.

"I will never leave thee, nor forsake thee" the
Lord promises (Hebrews 13:5). *"...The Lord uphold-
eth the righteous"* (Psalms 37:17). *"The eternal
God is thy refuge, and underneath are the everlast-
ing arms"* (Deuteronomy 33:27).

Once the eagle learns to soar, it rises to incredible
heights. When a storm cloud blocks its view of the
sun, the eagle goes higher, until nothing separates
it from the rays of the sun. Even when you and I
are separated and learn to fly, clouds and darkness
will come to overshadow us and block our view of
the Son. We must go higher. Get in the presence of
God. Shout and dance before Him. Let your spirit
soar above the problems and cares until nothing
separates you from the Sun of Righteousness. Just
keep going higher.

Every vessel, great and small alike, has to be
separated from the lump. The potter dipped the
string in water so that it would be moist and soft
and would do no harm as it accomplished the
necessary separation. The Lord will do all He can
to make the separation less painful. Cooperate
with Him. Know that He is doing a beautiful thing
in you.

Chapter Eleven

The Firing

Beloved, think it not strange concerning THE FIERY TRIAL which is to try you, as though some strange thing happened unto you.

(I Peter 4:12)

Once the vessel is molded and is separated from the lump, the next process it passes is the firing or heating. It is placed in an oven, or kiln, and baked. If you tried to put water into a recently formed vessel, it might hold it for a while. But then, the sides would weaken, and the vessel would begin to leak.

If you tried to put flowers into a recently formed

vase, the weight of the flowers would push the soft walls out and disfigure permanently the vessel. Fire hardens the vessel, so that the design will not be lost and the vessel may withstand rugged use. It becomes solid, firm, rigid, strong. A vessel that has not been fired yet is not useful. It is a vessel in one sense, but an unfulfilled vessel. It has not even begun to achieve the purpose for which it was formed. Every one of the "fiery trials" we go through works something glorious in us, though none of us enjoy it. When you see a person being greatly used of God, you know that they have been through some fires.

A vessel that has been through the fire is so tough it can hold hot liquids. It can even hold fire. It can take it. It has been tempered. The devil can throw anything against you when you have been through the fire, and it will not move you. You can survive anything. Nothing that people say or do to you will move you.

"The Fiery Trials" is not a popular subject. Everyone wants us to say that things are getting better and better, that everything will be fine. Optimistic messages are popular, but are they realistic? Jesus said, *"...the children of this world are in their generation wiser than the children of light"* (Luke 16:8). Economists are not optimistic about the future. Military leaders are not optimistic about the future. Government leaders are not optimistic about the future. Ecologists are not optimistic about the future. Do they know something we don't know? Enjoy life. It is not going to get any better here on this earth. Get ready for the fires.

So many saints are fine, until the heat is turned up. Then, they become like Mt. Vesuvius or Mount St. Helens. Things begin to rumble and an explosion is imminent. I was in the Philippines when Taal Volcano erupted. We went out to see it—the smoke, the spewing of ash, the rumblings etc.

A friend in Israel is an archaeologist. "When you are looking at what is supposed to be a piece of old pottery," he told me, "say to the salesman, 'Let me put this in water.' If they say 'no,' you can be sure they have patched it, repaired it. When placed in water, the patch will soften and fall out."

"If, on the other hand, they say, 'Sure! Go ahead!' you know that it has no crack, no holes, has not been repaired." You have to put it to the test. God has to put us through the fire.

Hasn't the clay been through enough? It has been dug up, dried out, beaten, sifted, mixed, kneaded, shaped and separated. But, it is not a finished product yet.

Isn't that a lot to endure? Well, let me put it this way: Wouldn't it be sad to go through the entire process and still not achieve usefulness? Yet, this is the point that many Christians decide they want to get off. They enjoy the Christian life, until the furnace heats up.

Many years ago Mother was teaching about the things that increase our anointing—prayer, fasting, reading the Word, and suffering trials and afflictions. We can understand and submit to the need to pray regularly, fast regularly, and read the Word of God regularly. But, submit to trials and afflictions regularly? None of us wants to do that.

Yet, James said, *"My brethren, Count it all joy..."* (James 1:2). We don't go around looking for problems. James said that we *"...fall into divers temptations"*. It isn't something we plan. We fall into it unknowingly. But, we are not overwhelmed by it. We recognize the hand of God in it and look forward to the enlargement God has promised: *"That the trial of your faith, being much more precious than of gold that perisheth, though it be tried with fire, might be found unto praise and honour and glory at the appearing of Jesus Christ"* (I Peter 1:7).

The same year that Mother gave that teaching I got typhoid fever in Pakistan and nearly died. I wasn't sure if I wanted to believe mother's doctrine or not. There is no doubt, however, that the trials and afflictions you go through make you strong. While others are stumbling, you can remain strong because you have been through the fire. You have been tested. If you are not going through the fire, get ready. You will. I guarantee it.

"*...ye shall have tribulation...*" (John 16:33). "*...we must through much tribulation enter into the kingdom of God*" (Acts 14:22). "*...we glory in tribulations...*" (Romans 5:3). "*Rejoicing in hope; patient in tribulation*" (Romans 12:12). "*...we told you before that we should suffer tribulation; even as it came to pass, and ye know*" (I Thessalonians 3:4). "*...your brother, and companion in tribulation...*" (Revelation 1:9). "*I know thy works, and tribulation...*" (Revelation 2:9).

All of us go through the fire. But, just as He appeared with the Hebrew children in the fiery furnace, Jesus is with you in the midst of your fiery trial. You will not be defeated, you will come through the fire with tremendous victory in your soul.

Don't fret over trials and hardships. Let God harden you, so that you can become a useful vessel. He turns up the heat. It has to get hotter and hotter. A lot of heat is needed for baking pottery. The hotter the oven, the faster the job gets done. A superficial baking is not sufficient. Who likes to eat half baked bread? God doesn't want you to be a half-baked Christian. He wants your strength to go deep. Well-baked pots can withstand a lot of rough treatment.

We have gone through a period when it has been

popular to be born again. It has been popular to be fundamentalists. It has been popular to be spirit-filled. That day is coming to a close. Not only will it not be popular in the future to be born-again and to speak in tongues, those who are openly born-again and spirit-filled will be hated and severely persecuted. Get ready for the fires of persecution. We need to stand and say as Job of old, *"Though He slay me yet will I trust in Him"* (Job 13:15).

This is the point in the process where some pots explode because they have hidden air bubbles. If the potter does not very carefully work out the air in the mixing stage, the vessel ends here in tragedy and destroys other vessels in the process. I have seen it happen.

When Peter went back to his fishing, he took six others with him. Any time a church has internal squabbles and someone gets mad at the pastor, and storms off, others will be destroyed in the process. Why do people blow up under pressure? Why can't they take the heat? Something is hidden in them that has not been dealt with in the formation process. They are an accident waiting to happen. The tragedy is that other, quite good, vessels will be destroyed by it.

I've seen people split a church and start another one, only to have someone come along and split that one. One pastor had a nervous breakdown and couldn't work when his church was split. He thought nothing of it when he split my father's church years ago. You can't afford to do it. You absolutely can't afford to do it. It will always come back to haunt you later. Mature sheep are never hurt by these tempests, but the little lambs are devastated. They get disillusioned.

In order to convince other members to split a congregation, a person must tell many bad things about the present pastor. Innocent lambs believe anything you tell them. They eat anything that looks good. They may be easily persuaded, but the process will lead them into eventual disillusionment. When they begin to examine the situation from a distance, they understand better the situation they left; and they get disillusioned with the person that pulled them aside. They get discouraged and lose faith in people. Many times they leave that church and backslide. They can't take it.

Jesus said, *"But whoso shall offend one of these little ones which believe in me, it were better for him that a millstone were hanged about his neck, and that he were drowned in the depth of the sea"* (Matthew 18:6). Those are hard words, but He meant it. Don't be guilty of destroying many other vessels just because of your hidden flaws.

When you are placed in the fire, we soon find out what you are made of. Everybody can rejoice in the midst of an anointed worship service. But, can you rejoice in the midst of the fire? When Saul got among the prophets, he started to prophesy. Anyone can do it when everybody else is doing it. But, when you are out there all alone in the real world and the devil comes against you, if you can still stand, if you can still have the victory, if you don't back up an inch, then that's a sign that you are getting somewhere in God. The fire is strengthening you.

God has a right to test you. He said, *"...he that endureth to the end shall be saved"* (Matthew 10:22). If you can't take the fire, He has a right to know it. He warns us against too much authority in the hands of *"a novice"* (I Timothy 3:6). He wants tested vessels. I saw vessels that could not take the fire. They went to pieces or burst their sides. They were thrown away. God's vessels must stand the test.

Trials come to solidify your position in God. When a trial is ended, drive a spiritual stake in the ground, and say, "I've grown that much in God. Look how far I've come. I've taken two giant steps." When the next trial comes and you weather it, mark off a few more steps and refuse to ever retreat. You are climbing a spiritual mountain into the realms of the glory of God. The fiery trials and tests cause you to be elevated into those realms.

Don't go back to what you had yesterday or last week. Start where you are now and go forward.

Don't take a single step backward. We have too many people who have compromised and gone backward. "Forward" is our battle cry.

Thank God for the fiery trials. The promise of God is, *"For our light affliction, which is but for a moment, worketh for us a far more exceeding and eternal weight of glory"* (II Corinthians 4:17). The tribulations, the hardships and the problems that God puts us through cause us to be strong.

In Psalm 4, David says, *"...thou hast enlarged me when I was in distress..."* (Psalms 4:1). Distresses enlarge us in God. A vessel that has passed through the fire is one step closer to effective service. We can have ministries just as great as anyone alive, if we are willing to go through the fires.

Don't run from the fiery trials. As God said to Paul, *"...My grace is sufficient for thee..."* (II Corinthians 12:9). He was severely tried. He said, *"I know whom I have believed, and am persuaded that He is able to keep that which I have committed unto Him against that day"* (II Timothy 1:12).

Abraham was severely tried. *"Where is the lamb for a burnt offering?"* Isaac asked him innocently (Genesis 22:7).

"God will provide..." was his answer (verse 8). He will also provide for you.

Chapter Twelve

The Painting

But we all, with open face beholding as in a glass the glory of the Lord, are changed into the same image from glory to glory, even as by the Spirit of the Lord. (II Corinthians 3:18)

But we have this treasure in earthen vessels, that the excellency of the power may be of God, and not of us. (II Corinthians 4:7)

I saw the potter paint the vessel. For years, when I preached this message, I left this part out. There were two reasons. First, I wasn't sure I understood exactly what God was showing me.

Secondly, I was so against the painting that was overtaking our godly women that I didn't want them to misinterpret what I was saying as an excuse to justify their vanity. I still believe, to this day, that God beautifies us with salvation and we don't need a lot of outside help. So, I always finished my message with the fire and let it go at that.

The truth is that a fired vessel, although attractive in a rustic sense, has not yet been beautified. It may be simply utilitarian, as in so many of the poor countries. But, God is not making just any old pot. He is fashioning vessels fit to enter the portals of glory.

We were taken to a factory in China where they make that gorgeous lacquerware. They showed us the process from beginning to end. Weeks are spent in the preparation of a single vessel. Some vessels actually took nearly three months to complete. We noticed with what care each step was carried out—each step important, each one adding to the finished product. I watched one man who worked with a fine sandpaper, hand polishing a beautiful vase. What care he took to ensure that the vessel was perfect. I was amazed. Some of those vessels sold for thousands of dollars.

At the very last position, I saw a man carefully painting the most beautiful Chinese scenes on the outside of a lacquerware vase. It is the painting that gives the vessel its character. As I stood there, transfixed, watching him, I got the revelation of what God is doing in us. He is putting the finishing touches on us. He is beautifying us to prepare us for His presence. He is doing that by stamping in us His character, His nature, His image!

They took us to a porcelain factory. I love Chinese porcelain. In a corner I saw all shapes and sizes of white porcelain vessels. I called to Mother and asked, "Which of these would you like to have?"

She said, "I don't like any of them."

I didn't like them either. They had no character, no personality. Later, however, when they took us to the sales room, and we saw the same size and type vessels, with the proper character and image on them, I wanted to buy them all. God is stamping His character in us.

The enemy of our soul is trying to get us to conform more to the image of the world. Jesus wants us to become more and more like Him, to take on His image and likeness. We are His ambassadors, His representatives. We need His seal and image upon us.

When the Holy Ghost descended on the day of Pentecost, it was not only to give us the nine gifts of the Spirit, but to stamp in us the character and the image of Jesus. He said, *"...every one that is perfect shall be as his master"* (Luke 6:40). It was to cause us to do the works that He did. He said,"...*the works that I do shall he do also; and greater works than these shall he do; because I go unto My Father*" (John 14:12). The fruits of the Spirit are a manifestation of the nature of Jesus. Thank God we are hearing more about the fruits these days. They are so much more important than the gifts of the Spirit.

The gifts of the Spirit began to function on the Day of Pentecost, when believers had been filled with the Spirit and spoken in other tongues. The gifts may come quickly. It takes some time, however, for love, joy, peace, longsuffering, gentleness, goodness, faith, meekness and temperance to grow upon the tree. But it is the fruit that shows forth the character of the tree. And if you want to have power with God, or if God begins to use you in a gift, and you want that gift to be deepened and enlarged, the only way to accomplish it is to permit the fruit of the Spirit to be manifested in your life.

When you allow the anointing of the Lord to bring joy and peace to your soul, and you begin to love, then we will be convinced of your gifts. Don't speak to me of the power in your life, if you can't get along with your brothers and sisters. Don't tell me that you have great power with God, when you still can't sit with those of other races, can't hug them and show them God's love. We can never grow in God unless we forget races and colors and personalities and sexes. You will only stand in power when the character of Jesus, the lover of our souls, shines out of you.

You can go into any mansion and recognize immediately a piece of pottery from China. It is distinctive. Once, we stopped in Vienna, Austria, on our way home from Israel. We were taken to the Aulsbad Castle, which belonged to a former head of state. As we walked through those stately rooms, it was so easy to spot each item that had been imported from China. They are so distinctive. They have China written all over them.

Moses went up to the mountain, where he met face to face with God. When he came back down, the image of God was so greatly stamped on his face he had to wear a veil over it. What did he look like? He looked like glory. His fellow men could not stand to look at Moses, because he looked like God.

You and I are to look just like Him and to have the glory and the anointing of God radiating upon our countenance. Jesus said, *"Let your light so shine before men, that they may see your good works, and glorify your Father which is in heaven"* (Matthew 5:16).

Several times, we have had the opportunity to visit Tibet, sixteen thousand feet in the air. On one occasion, four groups of ten foreigners each were there at the same time. Ten were from Australia, ten from Germany, ten from Austria and ten of us from the United States. We all looked pretty much the same. Yet, when four hundred and fifty Tibetan Buddhist monks passed by us, they did not stop before any of the other thirty and request prayer. They did stop in front of our ten, bowed their heads and requested (through motions) that we lay hands on them and bless them. They could sense something different about us, even though not one of us could speak their language.

When we walk down the street, people should know from the way we walk that we are different. They should be able to look upon our countenance and see Jesus. They should be able to listen to our conversation and know that we belong to Jesus. We should never be discouraged. We should never be depressed. We should never be angry and upset emotionally.

We are to look and act like Jesus and to have His character stamped and engraved within our souls. That being true, why then do most Christians seem to be going the other way, trying to be as much like the world as they can get by with and still hope to get into heaven? With so many, there is absolutely no way to identify them as believers. They are, in every sense, equal to the sinners. The only difference in them is they say they believe in Jesus. Can they be good representatives of the King of kings and the Lord of lords?

There was a time when America was honest and moral. The American tradition was the Christian tradition. But as the world gets worse and worse, we must turn further from its nature to Christ's. It is time that we stopped looking like the world and acting like the world and being like the world. Stop resisting the work of the Master Painter, Who is trying to paint a beautiful image on you.

On my way to North Carolina once to dedicate a church I had some other brothers with me in the car—among them a preacher from New York. We had a little time to kill and decided to stop at a flea market. We walked around and looked at the various exhibits. One of the vendors said to that brother, "C'mon preacher, buy somethin' from me." That brother had not said that he was a preacher. He didn't have a placard around his neck declaring, "I am a preacher." He didn't introduce himself or give his calling card. But, although he had done nothing to show that he was a preacher, that vendor saw something in him that made him know he was different from others. He said, "C'mon preacher. Preachers have plenty of money. C'mon and buy somethin' from me."

Wherever we go, people must be able to recognize that you have been with Jesus. Spirit-filled believers often recognize each other at a glance in crowded shopping malls etc. The first century religious leaders were amazed that the early believers were so much like Jesus. They could tell that they had been with Him (Acts 4:13). They talked like Him. They acted like Him. They had the same nature He had. Their response to life's hardships was the same as His. They couldn't hide. They were like Jesus. Peter, before the day of Pentecost, denied three times that he was Jesus' follower. But, he couldn't fool anyone. He was stamped with the image of Jesus.

We are not our own. We are in this world as His representatives. The most evident thing about us must be His image and glory. Chinese lacquerware is so beautiful that it draws your attention from a great distance. The Master's touch should be so notable in us. It is *"Christ in us"* that is the hope of glory. Let Him stamp His image on you today.

We used to sing that old chorus which ended with the words *"Stamp Thine own image deep on my heart."* If Christ's image is in you, you can never be the same. And those around you can never be the same. Some people will say we are "old fogies." Some will cry, "legalism." Others will be sure that this is "unnecessary in the twentieth century."

Several arguments have been used by Satan to get godly women to look and act like the world. "Even an old barn looks better when it's painted," said a famous preacher some time back. "The reason for the homosexual movement in the United

States is that women refuse to make themselves lovely," he declared.

Revival brings a desire to be like Jesus. We call it holiness. A return to holiness is a return to Christ-likeness. Those vessels that refuse to bear Christ's image will simply be unfit for His use. We are talking about Royal vessels here, fit for the King.

God may sit some well-known preachers on a shelf and raise up some nobodies to replace them, some nobodies who are willing to bear Christ's image.

Women, stop dressing to attract men. Start dressing to please God. Don't spend so much time in front of the mirror. Spend that time in something more worthwhile. You are beautiful to Jesus.

Men, stop dressing to attract women. Start dressing to please God. Don't look like you were poured into your clothes. It's time that we started to represent the King of kings and the Lord of lords. When we do, the anointing of God will be present and souls will be saved. The devil's kingdom will be shaken because we are like Jesus.

Chapter Thirteen

Marred Vessels

And the vessel that he made of clay was marred in the hand of the potter: so he made it again another vessel, as seemed good to the potter to make it.   (Jeremiah 18:4)

As the potter found vessels with serious flaws in them, he set them aside. Some had tiny holes in them. On some, the wall was too thin. Others had lost their shape etc. He wasn't discarding them in any sense. On the contrary, he would spend much more time and effort on these than on the others. They must go through the process again. But, as he encountered them, he laid them aside.

I have good news for anyone who feels "laid aside." God isn't finished with you yet. He hasn't lost the vision of what you can be. He will work you over again—if you will let Him.

When the original lump was finally depleted, the potter turned his attention to all the marred vessels. One by one, he placed them back onto the table and worked them all together into a central mass. Each one lost its individual identity again for a time. He had to knead the clay all over again, moisten it just right, put it back on the wheel and start the molding process over. When the vessels were formed, they had to be separated again.

Was it worth it? Yes! With their holes and twisted shapes the marred vessels were useless. It was double work for the potter, but he was determined to make something useful of the clay. He saw its value. Even a marred vessel can be refashioned.

Those marred vessels had not yet gone through the fire and been hardened. They were still soft. They could be remolded. The further along a vessel is in the process of perfection the more difficult it is to restore it, if it is damaged. Some, as we have seen, blow up and are destroyed. The softer the vessel is the easier it is to work with. Soft vessels can be restored. As long as your spirit is soft and tender toward God, there's still hope that God can bring out of you that which He desires. But, when you become cold and calloused and hardened toward the things of God, then God cannot do the work. The restoration depends on the softness or hardness of the material, not on the potter's ability.

Hebrews 6:4-6 tells us: *"For it is impossible for those who were once enlightened, and have tasted of the heavenly gift, and were made partakers of the Holy Ghost, And have tasted the good Word of God, and the powers of the world to come, If they shall fall away, to renew them again unto repentance; seeing they crucify to themselves the Son of God afresh, and put Him to an open shame."*

When you willfully turn away from God, you tie His hands. He hasn't lost the vision of what you can become. But, He cannot violate your sovereign will. You know people who have turned their back on God and are willfully running in the other direction. Willfully! God lets them be miserable; and they still run. At some point, a hardness comes into their spirit. God can still save them. He can save anyone. But, that hardness of spirit does not permit Him to do His work.

When I saw those vessels that had destroyed themselves in the heat of the fire, I asked the potter if he could do anything with them. "No!" he answered. "It is impossible to use that material again after it has become so hardened. They can only be thrown away."

When there is still a desire for God, it doesn't matter what mistake a person has made, how far he has fallen, Jesus is there to pick him up. If that person will just say sincerely, "Jesus, I'm sorry, forgive me," He picks him up again and starts molding something beautiful out of his failure. If you are a marred vessel, He is ready to put you back on the table. You'll have to be kneaded again and moistened again. You'll have to feel the pressure of His hands working on you. You'll have to be separated again. But if you are willing, He is too. As long as you are tender toward Him, there is hope. God even goes to the trash heap and picks up vessels that no one else sees hope for. He is a wonderful Savior and Restorer. "I can use that vessel," He says. "That's not worthless, as you imagined."

When I got desperate to be saved, I attended morning prayer meetings for three days. I attended the afternoon meetings. I attended the night meetings. For three days, I tried to give my heart to God. But, I couldn't feel a thing. I began to think that I had lost my final opportunity. For God said, "...*My spirit shall not always strive with man...*" (Genesis 6:3).

"You have played around with God too long," I said to myself. "Perhaps God will not hear your prayer."

That morning a brother asked me to kneel and

pray with him. I knelt in that ballroom in the Full Gospel Business Men's meeting in Seattle, Washington. And what joy flooded my soul, for I felt the presence of God. The floodgates of my soul were opened. The hardness began to go. Tears of sorrow and repentance came forth, as I cried out for God to have mercy on me. He can do it—when we are pliable in His hands.

God wants us to have a greater vision for broken vessels. Each of us has probably been marred in some sense. But, God didn't leave us. He didn't give up on us. He didn't lay aside His plan for us. Where would we be if God had no concern for marred vessels? Let's get that same vision for marred vessels.

Many people have been damaged by the enemy. Many are discouraged. Many have had their testimonies destroyed. Paul tells us, *"Brethren, if a man be overtaken in a fault, ye which are spiritual, restore such an one in the spirit of meekness; considering thyself, lest thou also be tempted"* (Galatians 6:1).

"Restore..." Someone has to do the restoration.

"Well, I think there's no hope for this one," people say. "There's no hope." "What hope is there?"

Oh, yes! There is hope! What baby ever learned to walk without falling down a few times. Do we just leave them there? No! They are learning. Pick

them up. Give them another chance. "Come on,
you can do it," we say. And they can and do.

God is in the restoration business. This is a year
of restoration. You will see many vessels, which
have been temporarily set aside, wonderfully
restored. Your backslidden loved ones will be
saved. Wandering sheep will be led back into the
fold. Many who have grown cold and indifferent
and forgotten God, will be restored to their first
love. Don't give up on them. Don't let the devil
make you feel that you've done all that you can do,
that there's no hope. He is a liar! There is hope!
There is a Restorer. His name is Jesus.

God didn't throw Adam and Eve away when
they sinned. He didn't discard them. From them
came the godly line of Seth. God wasn't finished
with them. He brought something good out of
their lives.

David transgressed and displeased God. But he
repented and remained soft before the Lord and,
from that transgression, God brought forth Solo-
mon, a great leader of His people. God did not
discard David.

Wasn't Jonah a marred vessel? Did God discard
Him? No!

We could go right down the line throughout the
Bible. God takes marred vessels and rebuilds and
refashions them into something beautiful.

If it doesn't happen, it's because men haven't

given Him the chance. He can do it. He wants to do it. Stop standing in His way and saying it is hopeless. Give Him the opportunity to show what He can do. He is the Master Potter.

Restoration takes time. Backsliders can't expect to jump back into the same level of anointing that they left. They have to go through the process all over again. It is more difficult to attain the same level the second time. It is a slow process. The potter must take care that the same flaws are not reoccurring, that the weaknesses are being properly addressed. Some become concerned that they are not attaining the same heights in God the second time. Be patient. God is not finished with you yet. You must move through the process in an orderly manner.

The important thing is you are being restored. Rejoice in that fact.

Chapter Fourteen

Hand-Made Vessels

*For we are His workmanship, created in Christ
Jesus unto good works, which God hath before
ordained that we should walk in them.*
                                    (Ephesians 2:10)

We're all hand-made vessels. No two of us are
exactly alike, just as no two snowflakes are alike,
no two fingerprints are alike, and no two voices are
alike. The voice, they say, is even more distinctive
than the fingerprints or the handwriting. And
now they have the DNA print—a genetic trait built
into each individual. A recent notorious case was
won by the prosecution here in Richmond by

presenting DNA experts, who testified of a unique trait in each cell of an individual that cannot be duplicated. None of us are alike. Identical twins are not identical. There is something about one that distinguishes him or her from the other.

The world's population is nearing five billion, more than has ever existed before on the face of the earth. Yet even comparing the billions who have lived and died and the five billion still living, no two have been made alike. God has taken two eyes, two ears, a nose and a mouth and made us all unique. How could any scientist ever doubt the existence of God? God made us.

Maybe you get upset because you're not like somebody else. Don't try to copy anyone else. Minister the way God made you. Prophesy the way God leads you. Pray for the sick the way God leads you. *"...There are diversities of gifts, but the same Spirit. And there are differences of administrations, but the same Lord"* (I Corinthians 12:4-5). We're different. We didn't come off an assembly line. We don't have "Made in Hong Kong" stamped on us. Sometimes we're guilty of trying to change a person's exuberant nature. Let the Holy Ghost redirect that energy. He has made each of us a unique person. We are hand-made vessels.

Something hand-made is so much more valuable! A hospital gave us nine thousand, five hundred yards of carpet. It was a wonderful blessing! But, that was factory-made carpet. I wouldn't trade you a car load of factory-made carpet for one hand-made by the Tibetans. They are one of a kind.

I hadn't been saved very long when a brother came to our camp who had a beautiful gift of the word of knowledge. I watched him, as he stood and called out individuals all over the congregation and told them what they were thinking, what they were praying. The response was so wonderful. I was very impressed. I said, "Lord, I want a gift just like that. That's the kind of ministry I want."

I was surprised when the Lord said, "It's not for you. I have something else for you."

God has a purpose in mind for you for which you are ideally suited. It is perfect for your personality, for your nature, for your disposition. He knows in what capacity you can bring the most glory and honor to the cause of Jesus Christ. It may seem peculiar to some, but it is of God. If you find the purpose for which God made you, your life will be totally changed. You will be a blessing to thousands of others.

One of the elderly sisters in our church, before she died in her eighties, had a very special ministry. She knew the birthdays of everyone in the church. When the day arrived, she sent them a card with a dollar or two inside. What a ministry. She never forgot. She was too old to travel around the world.

So, God gave her a peculiar ministry that blessed everyone. He has a special ministry just for you.

Isaiah, speaking of the work of the potter, said, *"...shall the work say of Him that made it, He made me not? or shall the thing framed say of Him that framed it, He had no understanding"* (Isaiah 29:16)? God knows what He is doing. Trust Him.

I bought two small hand-made bowls in Ecuador for five cents each. They were as valuable to me as souvenirs costing hundreds of dollars. The potter tried to make them alike. But, I could easily distinguish between the two. There were some definite differences. They were unique. They were hand-made. We have the Potter's hand prints indelibly stamped on us.

You can never be exactly like me and I can never be exactly like you. God intended it that way. You are a hand-made vessel. You are more valuable than the assembly-line variety. They may look pretty, but the skilled eye knows the difference. No two hand-made vessels are the same.

So, don't try to act like some other brother. Just be what Jesus made you to be. Don't copy somebody else's ministry. Let the Holy Ghost give you the ministry that He has for you.

Many people have tried to be just like the great evangelists, to copy everything about Oral Roberts, Kathryn Kuhlman, A.A. Allen or T.L. Osborn.

During the high point of Oral Roberts popularity, Dad knew a man, who so much wanted to be like Brother Roberts that he copied his mannerisms. He learned all of Oral Robert's sermons and preached them just like Oral Roberts did. In a tent meeting in Georgia one night, the man got so caught up in his imitation of Oral Roberts that, when he gave the invitation, he said, "If you come forward, Brother Oral will pray for you."

But, why copy someone else—no matter how great they are? Paul said, *"For we dare not make ourselves of the number...measuring themselves by themselves, and comparing themselves among themselves, are not wise"* (II Corinthians 10:12). Christ is our standard. We're to compare ourselves to Him. Let the Lord use your individuality! He made you unique for a purpose.

Elisha wasn't satisfied to imitate Elijah, as great as he had been. He wanted a double portion. He wanted to be twice the preacher. He wanted to do twice the miracles. He wanted to travel twice as far. He wanted to minister to twice as many people, with twice the power and anointing. And he got his desire, because he was pliable in God's hands.

Soon after I was saved, I said to Mother one day, "I don't want any of my sales ability to get involved in my preaching and ministry."

She laughed and said, "How can you separate the two? That's you."

God wants to use you. He has made you an individual vessels for His glory and for His honor. If you can stop fighting your individuality and surrender it to God, He will polish it up, remove the bumps and the bruises and the warts and the moles, and use what you have. You are a hand-made vessel.

We can't see the beginning from the end, as God sees. We don't know His entire plan. He has just shown us a little. We must trust Him. He loves us very much. He paid a great price for us. He knows what we can become. He knows tomorrow. He knows next week. He knows next month and next year. He understands the entire process. He knows how far we have already come and what remains to be done in us. Trust Him! He is still the Master Potter!

How long does it take the Lord? He said He could change nations in an *"instant"* (Jeremiah 18:7 and 9). It only takes the Lord an instant to do His work. We can't wait ten or twenty years. You can't sit for four years in a Bible School or seminary. You don't have time to meet all of man's requirements. Just go through the school of the Holy Spirit. Go through the school of hard knocks. Say, "Lord, here I am. Do Your work quickly in me." And the greater your desire to be used, the more quickly

He will be able to complete His work in you. I have seen the Lord take young men and women, work them over and, within a few short months and years, form beautiful vessels of them.

The further we move along in the development process, the more God expects of us. Fellow believers are in various stages of development. They may be from the same church. They may have attended the same seminary. They may have sat under the same teachers. Yet, they are in different stages of development. We need to recognize where they are and help them, instead of criticizing them. We cannot demand that they live on the same level as we do. But, God will change them quickly—if they allow Him.

Stop struggling against the work God is doing in you. Let Him perfect His desire in you today.

Oh God, in the Name of Jesus, I pray that You will move upon our lives. Make us vessels unto honor. I pray that You will so move upon us that we shall be pliable in Your hands, that we will not resist You, but that we will say, "Yes, Lord" to that which You would have us to do and that which You would have us to be. Help us to recognize that we are not our own. We have been dug out of the miry pit. We are Your love slaves.

Let Your hand be extended upon our lives. We want to allow You to make of us that which You desire. Let Your spirit and power hover over us, even now. Fashion us in the way You see best. Give us the gifts and the ministries that You want us to have.

Right now we allow You to work. Some of us are going through a sifting. Some of us are on Your table and are being beaten. Help us to respond quickly. Move mightily upon us, oh God.

Thank You for Your Word, and thank You for speaking to us from Your Word. Thank You for working in us. There is so much more that You desire to do in us. Make us willing, Lord.
Amen!

CALVARY PENTECOSTAL CAMP

10½ Weeks of
Spiritual Feasting
Every Summer
Beginning
The Last Week of June

with

3 GREAT SERVICES DAILY
- **11 A.M. Bible Studies**
- **3 P.M. Afternoon Services**
- **8 P.M. Evangelistic Services**

+

- **9 A.M. Youth Activities**
- **7 P.M. Youth Service**

Route 1, Box 365
Ashland, VA 23005
(804)-798-7756

MEET GOD AT THE CAMP!

Three new titles available

POWER IN YOUR HAND by Rev. Wallace H. Heflin—Everyday miracles through everyday people. God can use you! There is something very special about the laying on of hands—Your Hands! Discover how you are: An extension of God's hands: A point of contact with God's power: Able to do the works of God: A storehouse of God's power. ISBN 0-914903-64-0 Retail $6.00

WHO ARE WE IN CHRIST? by Harold McDougal—Who are we? What is our potential in Christ Jesus? We have only begun to tap into the vastness of our salvation. This book will open a new dimension of understanding concerning who we *really* are and *what* we really are. Who Jesus is and what He is directly relates to who and what we are in the Beloved. ISBN 0-914903-95-0 Retail $5.00

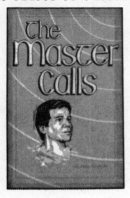

THE MASTER CALLS by Dr. Jerry Kirchner—What might happen to the average Christian if he would learn to hear the voice of God? What is preventing us from hearing His voice more in the twentieth century? What can you do to hear the voice of God more clearly? Does God ever take away from us things that we hold dear? ISBN 0-914903-70-5 Retail $5.00

Other exciting titles available

Two Books by Wallace Heflin

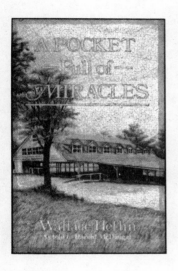

POCKETFUL OF MIRACLES by Wallace Heflin — Here is the amazing story of the founding and growth of Calvary Pentecostal Camp over a period of 35 years. You won't be able to put it down. A newspaper editor, considering the many things that God had done for them, decided that the Heflin family had "a Pocket Full of Miracles" You will agree once you've read this book. Enlarged edition. ISBN 0-914903-23-3 Retail $5.00

THE CHURCH AND THE BRIDE by Wallace Heflin — Who is the Bride of Christ? Israel? The Church? As Abraham's servant sought a bride for Isaac of the same family doesn't Christ deserve a bride who is like Him? Doesn't a spirit-filled Groom seek a spirit-filled Bride? Few people are familiar today with the Scriptural qualifications for becoming part of the Bride. Retail $2.00

The Church and the Bride

by Wallace Heflin

Exciting title available

From Dr. William A. Ward

ON THE EDGE OF TIME by Dr.
William A. Ward — This book is innova-
tive, exciting and electrifying! It is full
of provocative insights and keen escha-
tological truths gathered during more
than fifty-five years as an evangelist,
pastor and teacher. Over 350 pages.
Destiny Image.ISBN 0-914903-47-0
Retail paperback $10.00; hardback $15.00

Other exciting titles available

Two Books by Harold McDougal

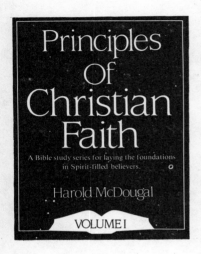

PRINCIPALS OF CHRISTIAN FAITH by Harold McDougal. — This book is the result of over twenty years of mission work overseas. This basic solid-truth study clearly lays the foundations for the Spirit-filled believer. Used in Bible schools and churches around the world, it's effectiveness has been proven over time. ISBN 0-914903-18-7 Retail $20.00

MASTER KEYS — SPEAKING IN TONGUES by Harold McDougal. — What is speaking in tongues? What is its purpose? When is speaking tongues out of order? Does speaking in tongues help me personally? Why is tongues so controversial? Does God want everyone to speak in tongues? Finally, there is a book in everyday language that clearly answers these and other apparently difficult questions about tongues. Compiling over twenty years of world-wide ministry with in-depth Bible study, Harold McDougal offers answers and guidelines that will help and encourage the seeking believer to function in his potential in the supernatural realm. Thought-provoking. Controversial. Truthful. TPB-112 p. ISBN 0-914903-65-9 Retail $5.00

21 ANOINTED AUDIO CASSETTE ALBUMS

by Rev. Wallace Heflin

1. God Can Use You (4 TAPE ALBUM) $18.00
2. The Holy Ghost and Fire
   (4 TAPE ALBUM) $18.00
3. Growing Into the Fullness of Christ
   (4 TAPE ALBUM) $18.00
4. Faith to Overcome (4 TAPE ALBUM) $18.00
5. The Anointing PART 1 (3 TAPE ALBUM).. $15.00
6. The Anointing PART 2 (3 TAPE ALBUM).. $15.00
7. Be Ye Holy (3 TAPE ALBUM) $15.00
8. Prayer, Fasting and Hearing the
   Voice of God (3 TAPE ALBUM) $15.00
9. Prophecy, Tongues and Interpretation
   (3 TAPE SERIES)........................ $15.00
10. Working for God (3 TAPE ALBUM) $15.00
11. Israel PART 1 (3 TAPE ALBUM) $15.00
12. Israel PART 2 (3 TAPE ALBUM) $15.00
13. The Blood of Jesus (3 TAPE ALBUM) $15.00
14. The End Time PART 1 (3 TAPE ALBUM).. $15.00
15. The End Time PART 2 (3 TAPE ALBUM).. $15.00
16. Victory in Jesus (3 TAPE ALBUM) $15.00
17. How You Can Receive from God
    (3 TAPE ALBUM) $15.00
18. A Message to the Church
    (3 TAPE ALBUM) $15.00
19. Prophecy and Prophets
    (3 TAPE ALBUM) $15.00
20. To Perfect the Saints (6 TAPE ALBUM) ... $25.00
21. According to the Promise
    (3 TAPE ALBUM) $15.00

You may
photo copy
form for
re-use

ORDER FORM

Return this form with your check or M.O. to Calvary Pentecostal Tabernacle,
Route 1, Box 365, Ashland, VA 23005

Phone Orders Call:
(804) 798-7756

QTY.	DESCRIPTION	UNIT PRICE	TOT. PRICE
	A Pocket Full of Miracles: *PB $5.00; HB $9.00		
	Principles of Christian Faith: $20.00		
	On the Edge of Time: *PB $10.00; HB $15.00		
	The Church and The Bride: $2.00		
	Master Keys: Speaking in Tongues: $5.00		
	Master Keys: Who Are We in Christ?: $5.00		
	Power in Your Hand: $6.00		
	The Master Calls: $5.00		
	TAPES		

Prices include shipping
* PB — Paperback; HB — Hardback

TOTAL DUE

Name _____
Address _____
City/State/ZIP _____
Date _____ Phone# _____